THE POCKET IDIOT'S GUIDE™ TO

More Not So Useless Facts

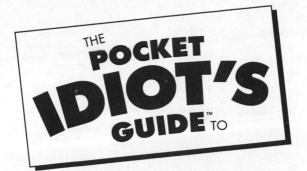

THE
**POCKET
IDIOT'S
GUIDE™** TO

More Not So Useless Facts

*by Dane Sherwood, Sandy Wood, and
Kara Kovalchik*

ALPHA
A member of Penguin Group (USA) Inc.

ALPHA BOOKS

Published by the Penguin Group

Penguin Group (USA) Inc., 375 Hudson Street, New York, New York 10014, USA

Penguin Group (Canada), 90 Eglinton Avenue East, Suite 700, Toronto, Ontario M4P 2Y3, Canada (a division of Pearson Penguin Canada Inc.)

Penguin Books Ltd., 80 Strand, London WC2R 0RL, England

Penguin Ireland, 25 St. Stephen's Green, Dublin 2, Ireland (a division of Penguin Books Ltd.)

Penguin Group (Australia), 250 Camberwell Road, Camberwell, Victoria 3124, Australia (a division of Pearson Australia Group Pty. Ltd.)

Penguin Books India Pvt. Ltd., 11 Community Centre, Panchsheel Park, New Delhi—110 017, India

Penguin Group (NZ), 67 Apollo Drive, Rosedale, North Shore, Auckland 1311, New Zealand (a division of Pearson New Zealand Ltd.)

Penguin Books (South Africa) (Pty.) Ltd., 24 Sturdee Avenue, Rosebank, Johannesburg 2196, South Africa

Penguin Books Ltd., Registered Offices: 80 Strand, London WC2R 0RL, England

International Standard Book Number: 978-1-59257-715-6
Library of Congress Catalog Card Number: 2007928986

09 08 07   8 7 6 5 4 3 2 1

Interpretation of the printing code: The rightmost number of the first series of numbers is the year of the book's printing; the rightmost number of the second series of numbers is the number of the book's printing. For example, a printing code of 07-1 shows that the first printing occurred in 2007.

Printed in the United States of America

Note: This publication contains the opinions and ideas of its authors. It is intended to provide helpful and informative material on the subject matter covered. It is sold with the understanding that the authors and publisher are not engaged in rendering professional services in the book. If the reader requires personal assistance or advice, a competent professional should be consulted.

The authors and publisher specifically disclaim any responsibility for any liability, loss, or risk, personal or otherwise, which is incurred as a consequence, directly or indirectly, of the use and application of any of the contents of this book.

Most Alpha books are available at special quantity discounts for bulk purchases for sales promotions, premiums, fund-raising, or educational use. Special books, or book excerpts, can also be created to fit specific needs.

For details, write: Special Markets, Alpha Books, 375 Hudson Street, New York, NY 10014.

Introduction

We approached this follow-up to *The Pocket Idiot's Guide to Not So Useless Facts* in much the same way we did the original. We all sat down together and played a game of mental mind-tag, trying to group together trivia and information in some interesting ways. As a result, we covered some subjects directly and dealt with others in more of a free-association fashion.

The purpose of this is two-fold: it not only allows us to cram a greater variety of material between the covers, but it should also help shake off some mental cobwebs as well. Take the category "Tigers." Until you get to that point in the book, you won't know whether the entries there reveal facts about real tigers, sports teams named the Tigers, tiger characters in movies, or some combination of those.

And we do that for a reason. Learning is all about tying things together. We might be just as likely to mention the Exxon tiger, the Cincinnati Bengals, or Diego from *Ice Age* as we would explain why tigers have stripes. This way, when you *do* come across a category that we've handled in a more direct way, your mind may wander to other closely related topics. Truly, it's that sort of association that helps the brain to "connect the dots." That's the cornerstone of problem solving and intelligence.

Yes, that sounds rather pretentious for a *trivia* book. But that's really the definition of trivia: it's the memorable details and connections that might slip the notice of the average person. You may not remember the number of home runs Babe Ruth hit, Joe Friday's badge number on *Dragnet*, or the year Pepin the Short was born. But if you know the answer to one, you know the answer to all: 714. It's easier for your brain to tie those answers together than to remember them separately. And connecting those facts helps save a few memory cells that might be used to absorb other things.

Finally, you may wonder why this book occasionally deals with certain specific subjects while eschewing ones that are more generic. Well, we covered many topics in the first book, and while 200 pages is a perfect length, it also provides us plenty of opportunities for additional volumes in the future. We're shooting for *Return of the Son of Yet Still More Not So Useless Facts, Part XII*. Hope you're still around then.

Dane, Sandy, and Kara
facts@ameritech.net

Acknowledgments

K. K. thanks Karl and Kurt Kovalchik, Mary Hamilton, Rhonda Porzadek, and M. G.

S. W. thanks his friends at the Stonesong Press, *Tidbits*, *mental_floss* magazine, and Borders Bookstore in Birmingham, Michigan.

D. S. gives thanks to Michael Buckley, Ellen Scordato, and Judy Linden.

Trademarks

All terms mentioned in this book that are known
to be or are suspected of being trademarks or
service marks have been appropriately capitalized.
Alpha Books and Penguin Group (USA) Inc.
cannot attest to the accuracy of this information.
Use of a term in this book should not be regarded
as affecting the validity of any trademark or service
mark.

Airplanes and Airports

Regular in-flight movie service began in 1961, when TWA Flight 40 treated passengers to the Lana Turner potboiler *By Love Possessed*. Today airlines carefully screen all motion pictures shown aboard their planes so that any references to aviation accidents can be edited out.

The first flight attendants were registered nurses hired in 1930 to treat airsick passengers. During World War II, when it became obvious that their services were needed elsewhere, the requirement that attendants be licensed medical professionals was dropped.

Beginning in 1929, the International Air Transport Association began assigning unique, three-letter codes to identify airports around the world. Some airports had already been using two-letter weather station codes, so an X was simply added to those designations (LAX, PHX, PDX, and so on).

The airport that handles more freight than any other worldwide is Memphis International in Tennessee. Not surprisingly, it's also the home of cargo giant FedEx.

Airport security is nothing new. In December 1972, after a rash of hijackings, the FAA gave airlines in the United States one month to install screening systems in their airports. The first metal detectors were 4-foot-long tunnels that originally had been designed for use in the logging industry to detect nails in lumber (which can ruin saws).

Why are flight crews so insistent that passengers have their seats upright and their tray tables stowed during takeoff and landing? It's a safety measure. In case of an emergency, it's important that aisles and rows be as clear as possible, and wayward chairs and trays would slow down evacuation procedures.

Alaska by Car

If you'd like to visit Alaska but don't care to fly, you can catch the Alaskan Highway, which is also known as the Alcan. The stretch of road begins in Dawson Creek, British Columbia, Canada, and snakes through the Yukon Territory, ending in Delta Junction, Alaska, about 100 miles south of Fairbanks.

Those who live in Alaska know that certain items are required packing before going on a car trip in the coldest parts of the state: extra-long jumper cables, an extra set of warm clothing, a snow shovel, and a block heater for the engine.

In the Lower 48, you see highway road signs warning you to watch out for humans, deer, and maybe ducks. But in Alaska, you need to watch out for bears, bighorn sheep, bison, caribou, moose, and even mountain goats. These creatures (and a few others) like to lick the salt off the roadways.

If you think Alaska has inexpensive fuel prices due to the large oil deposits there, you'd be incorrect.

Prices in Alaska are comparable to gas prices elsewhere in the United States. The actual fuel is a bit more costly due to transportation costs, but the consumer price is tempered by one of the lowest fuel tax rates in the United States.

Are you hoping to drive into Juneau, Alaska's capital city? Sorry, but that isn't an option. Water, glaciers, and impassible mountains form the city's boundaries, meaning that automobiles entering or leaving the city have to do so via ferry.

If pending legislation passes, those who drive from the Lower 48 to Alaska may be required to carry something with them that those who fly the same route won't: a passport. The only way to get to Alaska by automobile is to drive through Canada, so you may be required to show your passport at the United States/Canada border and again at the Canada/Alaska border.

Antarctica

If you ever get stuck for cash in Antarctica, it's helpful to know the site of the continent's lone ATM. It's located at McMurdo Station, a U.S. weather facility on the Hut Point peninsula. Additional fees may apply.

Emilio Palma was the first native-born Antarctican. He entered the world in 1978 as the son of two Argentine scientists who were sent there (most believe) to help the nation stake its claim to at least part of the continent.

Antarctica receives less precipitation on average than any other continent. While thousands of feet of ice cover parts of it, it's taken many, many centuries for this ice cover to build up.

The area of Antarctica is not limited to its land, but includes the ice that forms on and around it. As a result, the continent may be twice as large in the winter as it is in the summer.

American scientists and support personnel living in Antarctica don't typically earn any more than their domestic equivalents, but their income goes a lot further. Not only is there little to spend money on, but room and board are also included.

The Army

There are about five enlisted men for every officer in the U.S. Army. As of 2007, about 82,000 officers and 420,000 U.S. Army personnel were on active duty.

West Point, New York, is more than just the home of the U.S. Military Academy. Just like Kentucky's Fort Knox stores our nation's gold supply, the West Point facility is tasked with securing America's hoards of silver.

In the U.S. Army, there's a distinct difference between infantry groupings. A *squad* is a handful of soldiers. A *platoon* typically consists of three squads, and a *company* is usually made up of three platoons.

A *battalion* is commonly comprised of three companies, a *brigade* is three battalions, and a *division* is three brigades.

Four key promotions occurred during the run of the sitcom *M*A*S*H:*

- Season 5: Corporal Radar O'Reilly was (accidentally and temporarily) promoted to second lieutenant.

- Season 6: Major Frank Burns was promoted to lieutenant colonel and sent back to the States.

- Season 8: Father and First Lieutenant Francis Mulcahy was promoted to captain.

- Season 10: Corporal Max Klinger was promoted to sergeant.

During World War II, the U.S. Army reached its peak strength in 1945, with 8.25 million men and women actively serving. Only five years later, the numbers had returned to the more "normal" level of about 600,000.

Auto Logos

According to Catharine Durant, her husband saw the inspiration for the Chevrolet "bow tie" logo not on some French wallpaper (as legend has it) but in a newspaper ad while they were vacationing in Hot Springs, Virginia. Researchers believe the company responsible was an Atlanta-based coal supplier known as Coalettes.

The familiar Mercedes-Benz logo is neither a peace sign nor a propeller (that's BMW); it is a three-pointed star designed by Gottlieb Daimler to represent the dominance of his company's motors across land, on sea, and in the air.

Prior to 1933, the distinctive intertwined "RR" grille logo of Rolls-Royce was red. Upon the passing of founder Sir Henry Royce, the logo's color was permanently changed to black as a symbol of mourning.

What consumers call "hood ornaments," those in the automobile industry refer to as "mascots." These were originally designed as decorative alternatives to the traditional exposed radiator caps that stuck out in front of the hood. Among logos displayed in this fashion is the "Ram" icon of Dodge Trucks.

Franz Reimspiess was the engineer at Volkswagen who submitted the classic "VW" logo design in a 1930s company-wide competition. Reimspiess's winning entry earned him 50 deutschmarks, or about $35 U.S.

Cadillac redesigned its emblem in 1998, omitting the six ducks that had appeared in it since the company's inception. The merlettes had "come to life" in an advertising campaign for the automaker's ill-fated Catera, and the company wanted to distance itself from that failure.

Awards Cash

Medals and trophies are nice, but for many of us, everything comes down to cold, hard cash. So notwithstanding the intrinsic (or actual) value of crowns, rings, and potential endorsements, here's a rundown of the wallet-stuffing profit accompanying some famous awards:

- **Nobel Prize:** Varies, but recently has been 10 million Swedish kronor (approx. $1.5 million U.S.).
- **Pillsbury Bake-Off:** A Grand Prize of $1 million.
- **Westminster Kennel Club Dog Show:** No cash award.
- **National Spelling Bee:** $12,000 cash from Scripps and another $10,000 cash from other sponsors.
- **Pulitzer Prize:** $10,000, in 20 of 21 categories.
- **Guinness World Record:** $0 from Guinness (possible cash from sponsors, depending on the record).
- **Super Bowl:** In 2007, a winning player's share was $73,000; losers received half of that.
- *The Gong Show*: A check for $516.32 on the original NBC show; $712.05 on the syndicated version.
- **Miss America:** No actual cash, but a scholarship fund worth $50,000.

- **Olympic Gold Medal:** A $25,000 bonus ($15,000 for silver, and $10,000 for bronze).

Baby Development

Researchers aren't sure why the likelihood of having a left-handed baby increases with the number of ultrasounds the mother has while pregnant. A 2001 Swedish study revealed that males whose mothers had additional scans later in pregnancy had a 30 percent chance of being southpaws, compared to overall odds of 11 percent.

Babies are born with what is called a "stepping reflex." An infant held upright with his feet on a flat surface will automatically place one foot in front of the other as if trying to walk. This reflex disappears by about four months of age.

Scientists have identified certain characteristics that contribute to "cuteness": large, bright, forward-facing eyes; a large round head; and chubby cheeks. Some anthropologists believe that human babies developed these "cute cues" as a survival mechanism, compelling mothers to hold and nurture them.

At three months old, a baby has usually learned to recognize facial features. Even if Mother changes her hairstyle, Junior should still be able to identify her by her eyes and nose and the overall shape of her face.

Pediatricians long believed that smiling was a learned behavior that developed after six weeks, but modern research has shown that babies may smile earlier than that as a response to physical comfort. The brain stem, which doesn't respond to external stimuli, triggers the reaction.

Part of the reason that infant car seats are designed to face backward is that a baby's neck muscles aren't strong enough to support the head for about the first year of life. By facing away from the direction of travel, the baby's head is prevented from abruptly jerking forward in the event of a collision.

Baby Names

Madison was virtually unheard of as a first name for girls until Daryl Hannah's character used it in the 1984 movie *Splash*. In the film, she adopted the name after seeing a sign for Madison Avenue in New York.

According to Social Security Administration records, 1,022 girls born in America between 2000 and 2005 were given the not-so-unique name of Unique.

Because boxer George Foreman never knew his father, he made the decision to name all five of his sons George Edward Foreman. The heavyweight champ (and grill salesman) wanted them to always remember the patriarch of their family.

After it was announced that Gwyneth Paltrow had named her daughter Apple, Peaches Geldof (daughter of Sir Bob) wrote an open letter to London's *Daily Telegraph* pleading with celebrities to stop giving their offspring "ridiculous" names. Peaches, who has sisters named Fifi, Heavenly, and Pixie, revealed that her "weird" name has always haunted her.

As of this writing, four children in the United States are named Espn after the cable sports channel—two were born in Texas, one in Michigan, and one in Mississippi. In at least three of those cases, the mother admitted she'd let the father choose the name.

On a 2000 episode of MTV's *Cribs*, Sonny Sandoval revealed that his daughter's name was Nevaeh ("heaven" spelled backward). After word spread across the Internet, the name began to gain popularity, and by 2003, it was number 150 on the list of most popular names for newborn girls in the United States.

Backyard Games

The game of jacks started out as *dibstones* and was played using pebbles or even sheep's knuckles. When a player captured a piece, he would call out "I've got dibs!" which led to the contemporary usage of that expression.

The world's largest croquet complex is located in West Palm Beach, Florida, and covers 10 acres.

The jump rope game called Double Dutch is as old as the craft of ropemaking. In ancient Egypt and China, ropemakers walked backward, twisting the various strands of rope into uniformity, while runners jumped and dodged their way across the cluttered floors supplying the spinners with hemp.

Jarts, or lawn darts, were made illegal in the United States in 1988, after a few youngsters were seriously injured or killed by using them incorrectly. Lawn darts are even prohibited from U.S.-based auctions on eBay.

Badminton originated as a child's game in India called "battledore and shuttlecock." When British soldiers took the game back with them to the UK, it became a favorite of the Duke of Beaufort and eventually took on the name of his country estate, Badminton.

Hopscotch was created as a training exercise for soldiers during the Roman Empire. In order to improve their footwork, they had to traverse a 100-foot-long course in full armor.

In the fourteenth century, billiards—or the precursor to it—was played on outdoor lawns. Eventually, folks got tired of bending over, so they moved the game indoors and reduced it to the size of a tabletop. The green felt cover, still common today, is a nod to the sport's outdoor origins.

Bags

Many communities require grass clippings and yard trimmings to be disposed of in paper bags for collection. This is because the bags will decompose along with the vegetation at the compost facility.

Margaret Knight, an employee at the Columbia Paper Bag Company, was one of the first women in the United States to hold a patent. She invented a machine that folded and glued flat-bottomed bags, the type most grocery stores use today.

Plastic grocery store sacks, properly called "T-shirt bags," were introduced in 1977. Kroger and Safeway were the first two supermarket chains to replace brown paper craft bags with T-shirt bags.

In 1988, the Supreme Court upheld the right of law enforcement officials to search through a person's curbside garbage bags without a warrant.

Plastic dry-cleaning bags became controversial shortly after their introduction in 1958. Many parents, unaware of the suffocation danger inherent in the lightweight plastic, used the bags as leak-proof crib linings and mattress covers. The tragic infant deaths due to the plastic bags resulted in the warnings that are printed on all dry-cleaning bags today.

Dow Chemical introduced the Ziploc bag in 1968. The company test-marketed them in select U.S. regions the following year with outstanding results. Today it is estimated that the average American uses 40 of these bags per year.

Felix the Cat was created by Otto Messmer in 1919, but it wasn't until the "wonderful, wonderful cat" was retooled in 1954 by Dell Comics artist Joe Oriolo that his Magic Bag of Tricks was added to the mix.

Bald Is Beautiful

Yul Brynner was already losing his hair when he decided to shave it all off for his role as the king in the Broadway production of *The King and I*. He kept the bald look for the rest of his life, but wore wigs for subsequent film appearances that required hair.

Persis Khambatta was given the choice of either shaving her head or wearing a bald cap for her role as Ilia in *Star Trek: The Motion Picture*. She decided to go the razor route rather than endure the daily application of the gum and glue necessary to keep the bald cap in place.

Just in case anyone still believed that the lush carpet on his head was his real hair, comedian Rip Taylor removed all doubt when he pulled it off on a 1987 episode of *Super Password*. He stated that it was the first time he'd ever revealed his bald head on network television.

The directors of *V for Vendetta* only had one chance to get Natalie Portman's head-shaving scene in the can. As a precaution, several members of the crew volunteered to have their own heads shaved so that the lighting and camera angles could be properly adjusted before Portman went under the shears.

Telly Savalas was already quite bald by the time he landed the role of *Kojak* and shaved what hair remained for the hit TV series. He made sure, however, that his publicists "leaked" to the press that he regularly pruned his pate; otherwise, a full head of hair would quickly sprout up.

When Burt Reynolds filed for bankruptcy in 1996, it was reported that about $7,600 of his estimated $10 million in debts was owed to hair-replacement studios.

Bananas

The Velvet Underground featuring Nico was produced by Andy Warhol, who also designed the famous "banana" album cover. The original cover actually featured a removable banana sticker, along with the instructions, "Peel slowly and see." (See what? A flesh-colored banana, it turned out.)

The Banana Splits were originally going to be called *The Banana Bunch.* The last-minute title change for the Hanna-Barbera program meant that Kellogg, the show's sponsor, had to scrap several thousand boxes of cereal with the wrong name.

Charles Nelson Reilly was a highly respected acting teacher and director. He also spent much of the 1970s dressed as a giant banana in a series of commercials for the Bic Banana "ink crayon."

The most common banana eaten in the United States is the Cavendish variety. A bunch of bananas is properly called a "hand," and each individual fruit is a "finger."

The Chiquita Banana jingle was composed by the BBDO advertising agency in 1944. When the tune was being recorded, there were no maracas handy in the studio, so a box of paperclips was shaken in rhythm instead.

The Berkeley Barb caused some hubbub in March 1967 when it made a joking reference to smoking banana peels as a way to get high. The wire services picked up the story; soon the mainstream press was reporting this new legal high, and hippies were flocking to fruit markets in search of "mellow yellow."

Baseball

William Ellsworth "Dummy" Hoy was the first deaf person to play major league baseball and was responsible for the development of hand signals. Because he couldn't hear the calls as they were made, he asked the third base coach to raise his left arm to indicate a ball and his right arm for a strike.

The very first gloves used in professional baseball appeared in 1875. Flesh-tone material was chosen since the players were a bit shy about wearing them, it was considered "unmanly" to use protective equipment at that time.

Even though it's often referred to as "horsehide," official Major League baseballs are covered with alum-tanned, full-grained cowhide, primarily culled from Midwest Holstein cattle.

The Professional Baseball Umpire Corporation accredits only two umpire schools, both located in Florida. Tuition costs about $3,000 at either one.

In 2004, Columbia/Tri-Star Pictures entered into a marketing agreement with Major League Baseball in order to promote the film *Spider-Man 2*. The original plan called for first, second, and third bases to have the film's logo emblazoned on them, but a public outcry nixed that idea.

Umpire etiquette suggests that the ump should only brush off home plate while facing the backstop. That way he won't be presenting his backside to the majority of the fans in the stands.

Beer Advertising

The Clydesdale became the enduring symbol of Budweiser in 1933 when Prohibition was repealed. Even though horse-drawn carriages were no longer used to deliver brew, August A. Busch Jr. purchased a team of geldings and hitched them to a beer delivery wagon as a surprise for his father.

Former major leaguer Bob Uecker actually gained more fame as the perennial "loser" in a series of ads for Miller Lite. Not everyone thought of him as a Sad Sack, mind you. In 2006, he was forced to file a restraining order against a persistent stalker.

New York's Rheingold beer was famous for its annual "Miss Rheingold" competition, and Gothamites took this contest seriously. In the 1959 contest, 22 million votes were cast, making the New York "turnout" second only to the following year's presidential election.

Spuds MacKenzie, the "ultimate party animal" that pitched Bud Lite, was really a bitch. The English Bull Terrier, whose real name was Honey Tree Evil Eye, was a female dog forced to live a lie and pretend to be a male in front of the cameras.

That frosty mug filled with ice-cold beer you see on TV commercials is actually room-temperature beer with dish soap and salt added to keep a good foamy head. To give it that thirst-quenching look, glycerin is sprayed on the outside of the mug to simulate water droplets.

During the late 1970s, actor James Coburn was paid the then unheard of sum of $500,000 for uttering just two words in a series of beer commercials: "Schlitz ... Light."

Behind the Scenes of Reality TV

Simon, Paula, and Randy's reactions during the montage of the worst of the worst *American Idol* auditions are a result of clever editing. The three judges don't actually see any of the auditions until the contestants have been whittled down to the final 100.

A year after his stint on *Joe Millionaire*, series star Evan Marriott revealed to the press that much of the show had been staged, including the infamous "making out in the woods" scene, which the FOX sound effects department fabricated.

Some reality shows go the virtual route to locate potential contestants. Producers for *The Swan* and *The Biggest Loser* browse through Usenet groups online, hoping to find posts by women who admit that they feel "unattractive."

The real estate challenge in Season 1 of *The Apprentice* was a bit deceiving. After the episode aired, it was revealed that the party who rented the refurbished apartment from the winning team had actually signed the lease before the show's crew even arrived.

The contestants on *Dancing with the Stars* don't get to select their own music. The songs are picked by the producers, and the choices are often limited by whatever tunes they're able to secure the performance rights for.

Birds

Don't confuse the North American robin with the British robin. The bird they call a "robin" in England is smaller than our U.S. variety and is a symbol of Christmas, not a harbinger of spring.

Robert Stroud was known as the "Birdman of Alcatraz," but he actually only kept birds when he was incarcerated at the Federal Penitentiary at Leavenworth. Officials at Alcatraz nixed his avian hobby.

Atlanta is home to three professional sports teams named after birds: the NFL's Falcons; the NBA's Hawks; and the NHL's Thrashers, which is named after the state bird, the Brown Thrasher. The city's fourth team, MLB's Braves, don't fit the same mold—but a stylized feather *was* once used as the team logo.

Smaller, lighter birds that spend most of their time in trees generally hop when on the ground, while larger birds run. In each case, it's a matter of what type of locomotion moves the bird most efficiently and uses the least amount of energy.

Due to the nature of the vulture's diet, its extra-strong stomach acid is designed to kill virtually any type of bacteria or virus.

The melodiousness and versatility of a bird's voice is a product of evolution. Birds that spend most of their time in trees need voices that carry in order to communicate and attract mates, so they have highly developed vocal muscles.

No natural bird sounds are heard in Alfred Hitchcock's 1963 horror classic *The Birds*. All the chirps, squawks, and screeches were electronically generated for maximum terrifying effect.

Bonanza

The map of Virginia City, Nevada, that burned during the opening credits of *Bonanza* was turned sideways so that East was at the top instead of North.

Michael Landon was the only main male cast member who had a full head of hair. However, Landon's locks had actually gone prematurely grey by the time he was 20 years old. The chestnut brown color he sported on *Bonanza* was thanks to Clairol Ash Brown.

Dan "Hoss" Blocker was famous for ruining takes because he'd frequently forget to remove his Rolex wristwatch (an accessory that wouldn't be present in the Old West) before filming a scene.

Pernell Roberts had been a staunch supporter of civil rights since his childhood in the segregated South. When his six-year contract with *Bonanza* was up, he refused to renew it because he thought the show perpetuated racist and sexist stereotypes.

The 10-gallon hat that was Hoss's trademark was originally plopped on Dan Blocker's head as a joke when he was first being fitted for his *Bonanza* wardrobe. However, the oversized chapeau so suited the 6'4" actor that it soon became his trademark.

Lorne Greene as Ben Cartwright was featured on a Canadian postage stamp in 2006 as part of a "Canadians in Hollywood" commemorative series.

Watch carefully during the opening credits on the earliest black and white episodes of *Bonanza*. As the Cartwrights gallop their horses down a trail, the dirt beneath them reveals the unmistakable signs of tire tracks from the camera truck that's filming them.

Bones of the Body

The three smallest bones in the human body are found in the middle ear: the *malleus*, the *incus*, and the *stapes* (better known as the *hammer*, the *anvil*, and the *stirrup*).

Wrist fractures are the most common broken bone injury in people under the age of 75. After that, a much more problematic bone— the hip—moves into first place.

Infants are born with up to 300 "soft" bones, many of which harden and fuse together as the baby grows. As an adult, a typical human adult's body contains 206 bones.

Stuntman Evel Knievel earned a place in the record books by having broken 35 bones during his career. He's suffered more than a dozen surgeries to repair them, including one to rebuild his pelvis after he shattered it during a motorcycle jump attempt in 1967.

The tingling you feel when you hit your "funny bone" occurs when the ulnar nerve hits the humerus bone in the arm. It's uncertain whether the "funny bone" nickname came about due to the strange sensation, the name of the bone itself, or both.

Men and women have the same number of ribs: 24. Fourteen *true ribs* connect to the spine and the sternum, six *false ribs* connect to the spine and the bottom true rib, and four *floating ribs* connect only to the spine.

The Brady Bunch

The word "sex" was only uttered once during the four-year run of the show. Cousin Oliver blurted it out in the final episode of the series when Mrs. Brady had difficulty explaining the mating habits of rabbits.

Sam the Butcher had a last name, though it was only mentioned once during the series: Franklin.

The Peppermint Trolley Company, who sang *The Brady Bunch* theme song for the first season of the series, also performed the theme song to the long-running sketch comedy series *Love, American Style*.

Watch Bobby's hair color change over the course of the series. Mike Lookinland's hair was naturally a reddish-blond, but the producers experimented with a number of different colors each season in order to make the youngest Brady's hair color match that of his brothers.

The show was originally entitled *The Bradley Brood*, and Gene Hackman had been the producers' original choice for the role of patriarch Mike Brady. However, the network felt Hackman was too much of an unknown and went with Robert Reed instead, who'd had a successful run on TV's *The Defenders*.

Florence Henderson wore a wig throughout the first season of the show because her own hair had been cropped short for a role in her first feature film, *Song of Norway*.

That lisp of Cindy Brady's was very real and so endearing that Sherwood Schwartz had an episode written around it. Susan Olsen had the speech impediment surgically corrected as an adult.

Bridges

San Francisco's Golden Gate Bridge is painted a specific shade known as International Orange. The bridge's designers felt that the orange hue blended best with the warm colors of the land in the area and the cool colors of the sky and sea.

On May 30, 1883, with mobs of people still crowding the promenade of the newly opened Brooklyn Bridge, a woman tripped while walking and screamed. Others interpreted her scream to mean that the bridge was collapsing, and the ensuing stampede resulted in 12 deaths and scores of injuries.

The single busiest international land border crossing in North America is the Ambassador Bridge, which links Detroit, Michigan, and Windsor, Ontario. When the bridge first opened, it became a fad for couples to exchange their wedding vows in the middle of it, until it was pointed out that the area was technically a "no-man's land," neither America nor Canada, and the marriage might not be valid.

Shortly after the Tacoma Narrows Bridge opened in 1940, it earned the nickname "Galloping Gertie" due to the way it undulated in the wind. On November 7 of that year, owners of a nearby camera shop got word that the bridge was in trouble due to high winds and captured footage of the bridge as it twisted, buckled, and ultimately collapsed.

The London Bridge was built in 1831, but due to increased traffic, it was falling down by 1962. On a whim, the local government put the bridge up for sale. To their surprise, they found a buyer! Robert McCulloch, the founder of Lake Havasu, Arizona, paid nearly $2.5 million and had the bridge moved to Arizona brick by brick. It still stands in Lake Havasu.

It's no surprise that Lancaster County, Pennsylvania, is home to more covered bridges than any other area of the United States. The protective covers over the bridges keep them free of snow and rain so that the horse-powered carriages of the Amish can safely cross, no matter what the weather.

British Terms

If you plan to rent a car while visiting the UK, you might be asked whether you prefer an *estate wagon* (station wagon) or a *saloon* (sedan). Stow your luggage in the *boot* (trunk) and ask how to pop the *bonnet* (hood) in case of engine trouble. When the agent asks you what the *clock* says, don't give him the correct time; he's referring to the odometer reading.

Even if you're wearing a fanny pack, don't refer to it by that name, as *fanny* has an entirely different (and much more personal) meaning in England.

 Eating in a restaurant presents another challenge. If you ask for *jelly*, you'll get gelatin.

A *joint* is not something you smoke; it's roast beef. If you're a vegetarian, look for *marrow* (squash) and *aubergine* (eggplant) on the menu, not *gammon* (ham).

Are you traveling with a baby? You'll want to remember that in Britain, a crib is a *cot*; a pacifier is a *dummy*; a diaper is a *nappy*; and a stroller is a *pushchair*.

While relaxing at the *pub* (bar), you might enjoy a *packet of crisps* (bag of potato chips) with your *pint* (glass of draft beer). Perhaps you'll while away the time playing *naughts and crosses* (tic-tac-toe) while puffing away on a *fag* (cigarette).

Don't be offended if a male British friend offers to *knock you up*; it simply means he'll stop by your place to collect you for whatever activity you have planned.

Candy Brand Names

Three Musketeers originally made a bit more sense as a name for a candy bar. When it was introduced in 1932, the bar was divided into three sections: one vanilla, one strawberry, and one chocolate. The latter proved the most popular flavor, so the candy was later changed to all chocolate.

Forrest Mars and Bruce Murrie were the M's behind the sweet treats known as M&M's.

The official explanation for the name of the Baby Ruth candy bar has always been that it was named after Grover Cleveland's daughter. However, she died 17 years before the confection was introduced. It is believed that Curtiss Candy perpetuated the Cleveland story when Yankee slugger Babe Ruth sued for royalties.

Tom Henry of Arkansas City, Kansas, invented a candy bar bearing his name in 1919. He later sold the recipe to the Curtiss Candy Company, which changed the name of the treat to "Oh, Henry."

The 1975 book *Looking for Mr. Goodbar* wasn't specifically named after the Hershey candy bar, which first appeared in 1925. The title referred to a single woman looking for a "good man" as she frequented a singles bar.

The Snickers bar was named after a horse owned by the Mars candy family.

The $100 Grand candy bar was originally known as the $100,000 bar. In June 2005, Hot 102-FM in Lexington, Kentucky, was sued by a "lucky caller" who thought she'd won $100,000 from the radio station, only to be told that the real prize was just a $100 Grand bar.

Card Games

Does "gin rummy" have anything to do with the alcoholic beverages gin and rum? Almost. While the origin of "rummy" is uncertain, an early-twentieth-century variation of the game became known as "gin," as a bit of a play-on-words about booze.

When someone slides you a deck of cards and asks you to cut, it's considered poor etiquette to handle the cards *other* than to do the actual "cutting" of the deck. The dealer should be the one to restack the cards before beginning to deal.

Two of the most popular specialty card games of recent memory have foreign names: Mattel produces *Uno* (Spanish for "one"), while Parker Brothers markets *Mille Bornes* (French for "a thousand mileposts").

The Ace of Spades typically has a larger "pip" (marking) than any other card and may include the manufacturer's name as well. This dates back to the days when this card was the one most commonly stamped to indicate that all applicable taxes had been paid.

Best known today for their video games, the Nintendo Company was founded in 1889 as a Japanese maker of playing cards. The brand didn't get into the electronics business until the mid-1970s.

Most experts in the five-card draw variation of poker recommend that you draw three cards if you have a single pair after the initial deal. The odds of improving your hand are greater by getting three new cards than by holding a "kicker" card.

Carpets and Rugs

Before it became the carpet capital of the world, Dalton, Georgia, was the nation's bedspread capital. Handmade chenille bedspreads were a local craft whose demand grew so quickly that manufacturers were forced to mechanize the process. The tufting technique used to make the spreads was eventually adopted to make looped yarn carpeting.

Saxony is carpet whose tufts are sheared to a low, smooth pile height for a uniform and formal look. Frieze is carpet in which the yarns are left longish, for a comfortable, casual appearance. Berber is made of level fabric loops, which makes for a dense surface suitable for high-traffic areas.

Technically speaking, an Oriental rug is one that has been hand-knotted in Iran, China, India, Russia, Turkey, Pakistan, Tibet, or Nepal. A Persian rug must have been made in Iran in order to be authentic.

The famous red carpet used at the annual Academy Awards is actually more of a burgundy shade. The rug starts out white and is dyed a secret shade of cayenne over the course of five days.

In the film *Cleopatra*, Elizabeth Taylor performed some magic that even the Queen of the Nile couldn't conjure. In the scene where she is rolled out of a large *rug* before Julius Caesar, which Cleopatra really did, she's wearing sandals. When she stands, however, her footwear mysteriously change to high-heel shoes.

Maids, butlers, and other "below stairs" staff at Buckingham Palace are not allowed to walk down the center of the carpet in any of the miles of corridor. They are required to traverse along the edges and must never look a member of the Royal Family in the eye should they pass by.

Cats

Cats, giraffes, and camels are the only mammals that walk by moving the two legs on one side together, then the other. Walking this way propels the animal in a diagonal direction, uses a minimum of energy, and helps ensure speed and silent movement.

Cats, like camels, were originally desert animals; over time, evolution has caused the cat to require less water than most other mammals. The cat's limited water intake makes for highly concentrated and foul-smelling urine.

Cats watch our eyes to learn to place themselves in front of whatever we're trying to read. It's also the reason that "friendly" cats seem to zero in on visitors who are not "cat people." Cats take the lack of interest and the absence of eye contact as a friendly overture and often an invitation to hop up on that person's lap.

Of the world's cat population, only 5 percent are truly pure white. Of true white cats with two blue eyes, it is estimated that two thirds to three quarters are born deaf.

Domestic cats rarely meow at one another; they communicate instead by using their ears, eyes, body position, and tail. They most commonly use their vocalization skills in order to communicate with humans, who are too stupid to read their body language.

Despite their reputation as finicky eaters, cats respond more to their food's texture and temperature than its flavor. Cats prefer that their food be at least room temperature, and will usually turn up their nose at food fresh from the fridge.

Housecats aren't afraid of water and are actually excellent swimmers. The reason they don't like being submerged in H_2O is because it's such a chore to lick themselves dry afterward. If Fluffy doesn't have to get wet to catch her food, then there's no real purpose in going for a swim.

Centenarians

Producer Hal Roach worked with scores of legendary comedians including Laurel and Hardy, the Our Gang kids, and Abbott and Costello. He outlived most of them, too, before he passed away in 1992 at the age of 100.

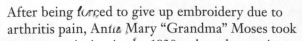

After being forced to give up embroidery due to arthritis pain, Anna Mary "Grandma" Moses took to painting in the 1930s when she was in her seventies. Far from being at the end of her career, Moses' continued work earned her near-universal praise. She published an autobiography at age 91 and passed away a decade later.

Amos Alonzo Stagg revolutionized the game of football, bringing innovations ranging from helmets to huddles. The charter member of the College Football Hall of Fame finally found his way to the end zone in 1965. He was 102.

Bob Hope was five years old when his family emigrated from England and settled in Cleveland, Ohio. He performed USO shows for 50 years, beginning in World War II and continuing through the Persian Gulf War. Hope passed away in 2003, just a few weeks after topping the century mark.

Born Isadore Baline, songwriter Irving Berlin adopted his new name after it was misprinted that way on the first sheet music he ever published. The man behind legendary songs like "White Christmas" and "God Bless America" was 101 when he died in 1989.

While many members of the Kennedy clan were lost in the prime of their lives, the matriarch of the family—Rose Kennedy—lived to the ripe old age of 104. She survived her husband Joe; sons Joe Jr., John, and Robert; and daughter Kathleen.

Checks

If you win the lottery, can you actually cash that giant check they present to you? If it has the account owner's name, the date, the words "Pay to the order of" followed by the payee's name, the dollar amount in numerical and written form, the name, the city and state of the bank where the account is held, and the signature of the account owner, it's a valid instrument.

That odd string of characters across the bottom of a check is the MICR (Magnetic Ink Character Recognition) line. It allows automatic sorting machines to "read" the account and the bank on which the check is drawn so that it can be forwarded to the proper institution.

The system of banks allowing customers to write paper checks originated in Holland in the 1500s. Amsterdam was a major international shipping port and a convenient place for traders to deposit their money rather than carrying it with them.

The use of checks in the United States didn't really take off until the 1920s. Prior to that time, paying with something other than cash had a certain stigma attached to it, as it was a sign that the person couldn't afford to pay his debts. Luckily, it became fashionable to spend, spend, spend during the Roaring Twenties.

The majority of forged or fraudulent checks are drawn on accounts that are less than three months old, which is why many merchants have stopped accepting low numbered checks. This is also why, when you open a new account, the first check number is "101" and not "1."

Cheerleading

A favorite cheerleading tune, the video for Toni Basil's number one hit song "Mickey" included real-life cheerleaders. Toni's uniform was real as well; the "LVH" patch stood for Las Vegas High, where she was on the squad in the early 1960s.

Many of the stunts performed in the 2000 film *Bring It On*, including the fly-overs and the basket tosses with head-over-heels rotation, are illegal in competitions at the high school level because of safety concerns.

The first organized chant occurred during a football game at Princeton in the 1880s:

> *Rah, Rah, Rah!*
> *Tiger, Tiger, Tiger!*
> *Sis, Sis, Sis!*
> *Boom, Boom, Boom!*
> *Aaaaah! Princeton,*
> *Princeton, Princeton!*

The Washington Redskins cheerleaders are the oldest active cheerleading organization in the NFL. The First Ladies of Football made their debut as the Redskinettes on September 30, 1962.

Cheerleading was an all-male sport until World War II summoned the fittest men overseas. When the war ended, co-ed squads became the norm, as the teams could perform more dramatic stunts using the lighter-weight female cheerleaders.

The quintessential cheerleading jump, the Herkie, was invented by and named for Lawrence Herkimer. Herkimer developed the move, which features the right arm thrust upward and one leg bent behind, in order to gain more height in his jumps while serving on the Southern Methodist University cheerleading squad.

Cheese

California is poised to overtake Wisconsin as America's top cheese-producing state within the next few years. However, America's Dairyland is quick to point out that Wisconsin is home to approximately 600 varieties of cheese, while California only offers a choice of 250.

Traditional mozzarella is made from the milk of water buffaloes, but in today's world, the gooey cheese is more commonly made from cow's milk. Thanks to America's love of pizza, mozzarella represents 30 percent of the nation's cheese production.

Tiny armies of bacteria expelling gas are responsible for the holes in Swiss cheese. Interestingly enough, the USDA has regulations in place regarding hole size and what grade the cheese is as a result.

Do ewe love bleu cheese? The variety known as Roquefort is made from sheep's milk and is ripened in caves in the south of France.

President Richard Nixon's favorite lunch treat was cottage cheese with ketchup.

Did people really once think the moon was made of green cheese? Not exactly. In John Heyward's book *Proverbs*, he suggested the concept, but he meant "green" cheese as in "not yet ripened" cheese, not the color green. And yes, the moon (with its craters) does resemble a roundish hunk of Swiss!

How can you tell if your foul-smelling-to-begin-with wedge of Limburger cheese has gone bad? It will smell like ammonia.

Chicago

The fountain shown in the opening credits on TV's *Married ... with Children* is the Clarence Buckingham Memorial Fountain located in Grant Park between Michigan Avenue and Lake Shore Drive in Chicago. Until 1994, a computer in Atlanta, Georgia, controlled the lights and water in the display.

Every year for St. Patrick's Day, the Chicago River is dyed emerald green. It takes 40 pounds of dye to turn the river green for about 5 hours, a tradition that started in 1961.

Many of John Hughes' teen comedy films (including *Sixteen Candles* and *Pretty in Pink*) were set in Shermer, Illinois, a northern Chicago suburb that doesn't exist on the map. Hughes' hometown of Northbrook was originally called Shermerville.

Oprah Winfrey first came to Chicago in 1984 to cohost WLS-TV's *AM Chicago*. After one month, the show's ratings surpassed that of Phil Donahue's, and one year later, the show was renamed *The Oprah Winfrey Show*.

Peter Cetera, lead singer for the band Chicago, actually developed his signature style of singing through a clenched jaw as a fluke. While attending a baseball game at Dodger Stadium in 1969, the longhaired Cubs fan attracted unwanted attention that resulted in a broken jaw which had to be wired shut.

The official FAA code for Chicago's O'Hare airport is ORD, but unlike popular rumor, the letters don't stand for "O'Hare—Richard Daley" after the city's long-serving mayor. Until 1949, the airport was known as *Or*chard Field and was still known as such when the three-letter FAA codes were handed out.

Chickens

Farmers are prohibited by law from using any artificial color enhancers in their chicken feed. However, they can (and do) feed their chickens marigold petals to give their hens' egg yolks that pleasing yellow hue.

The "chicken" version of the song "In the Mood" was recorded by a fictitious group called The Henhouse Five Plus Too. The man behind the recording is one of the best-known names in the novelty song world: Ray Stevens.

Are you confused by the different poultry designations in your supermarket's meat locker? A bird designated as a broiler or fryer is between 7 and 13 weeks of age. Roasters are three to five months old, and their meat is more tender and flavorful. Stewing chickens are older still, and while their meat is tasty, its toughness makes it best used in soups or stews.

There is no health benefit in brown versus white eggs. Hens with white feathers and white ear lobes produce white eggs. Brown eggs come from hens with red or brown feathers and red ear lobes. Brown eggs often cost more because the hens that lay them—Rhode Island Reds and Plymouth Rocks—are larger birds and eat more feed.

In chicken terminology, a *pullet* is a young female; a *hen* is a female that has laid eggs for at least six months; a *cockerel* is a young male; a *rooster* is a mature male; and a *capon* is a castrated male.

Natives of Marietta, Georgia, frequently give driving directions in relation to "The Big Chicken." The giant mechanical bird was originally erected in 1963 at the corner of Georgia Highway 120 and U.S. Highway 41 to advertise Johnny Reb's Chick, Chuck and Shake Restaurant.

Varicella affects humans, not chickens. This disease is called "chicken pox" because it was considered weaker than other pox diseases like smallpox.

The dark meat of a chicken contains more myoglobin, which is found in the muscles used for sustained activity, such as walking. Chickens rarely use their flight muscles, which is why the breast meat is white.

Children's TV

The Mickey Mouse Club and *Captain Kangaroo* both premiered on television on the same date, October 3, 1955. While the original *Club* only lasted three seasons, Bob Keeshan's *Captain* remained on the air until 1992.

Before they collaborated on such kiddie favorites as *H.R. Pufnstuf* and *Land of the Lost*, brothers Sid and Marty Krofft produced a nude puppet show in 1960 called "Les Poupee des Paris."

Morgan Freeman, Rita Moreno, and Bill Cosby were all regulars on the PBS series *The Electric Company*. At the beginning of each episode, Moreno's voice was heard yelling, "Hey you guys!"

Capitol Records originally created Bozo the Clown as one of the characters for their line of "record readers," a series of 78-rpm records accompanied by a picture book. The dialog from the record was also printed in the book so children could read along as it was spoken.

Those sweaters that Fred Rogers changed into at the beginning of every episode of *Mister Rogers' Neighborhood* were all hand-knitted by his mother. When Mr. Rogers met Koko, the famous sign-language gorilla (who watched his show daily) in 1998, one of the first things the giant primate did was unzip Fred's sweater.

Ernie Coombs arrived in Canada in 1963 to work on a children's TV show with Fred Rogers. When Rogers returned to the States, Coombs stayed in Toronto, and CBC gave him his own show. *Mr. Dressup* ran from 1967 to 1996 and became as beloved in Canada as Mr. Rogers was in the United States.

Chinese Food

The title of the Paul Simon 1972 hit single "Mother and Child Reunion" was adopted from the name of a chicken-and-egg dish he spotted on the menu of Say Eng Look, a Chinese restaurant in the Chinatown section of New York City.

In China, "pork" is synonymous with "meat." The Chinese do eat beef, but because cattle are more valued as work animals, most of their dishes are made with swine.

Chop suey is strictly an American concoction. Chinese immigrants who worked on the railways would cook together whatever vegetables and meat they had available. The name comes from the Mandarin phrase "tsa sui," which means "mixed pieces."

When 110 different players claimed second prize in the March 30, 2005, Powerball drawing, lottery officials suspected some type of fraud. However, it turned out that all those winners had played numbers they'd found in fortune cookies.

During the Chou Dynasty, China struggled to feed its people. What little forestation the area had was cleared for agricultural purposes. Traditional Chinese cuisine evolved in reaction to the wood shortage; because baking and boiling would take too long (and thus too much firewood), food was cut into small pieces and quickly stir-fried.

The cardboard cartons with metal handles that we associate with Chinese food carryout were originally used as oyster pails along the Eastern seaboard. In the 1940s, the burgeoning Chinese restaurant market discovered that the oyster pails made convenient and distinctive containers for their carryout wares.

The Circus

John Ringling and his wife started spending their winters in Sarasota, Florida, in 1909. They fell in love with the area and in 1927 made it the winter headquarters of their circus. Ringling used his elephants to help with construction as he developed a commercial and residential center in the area.

John Philip Sousa's "Stars and Stripes Forever" is known as the Disaster Song in the circus world. It is only played in case of emergency as a way to signal to circus personnel that something is wrong without alarming the audience.

Professional clowns unofficially "trademark" their faces by sending close-up photos of themselves in full makeup to the Department of Clown Registry in Milwaukee. The clown submits a close-up photo of his face, and an artist painstakingly recreates it using acrylic paints on a goose egg, where it is kept "on file."

Romanian gymnast Teodora Ungureanu was overshadowed by Nadia Comaneci's popularity at the 1976 Montreal Olympics, despite winning two silver medals and a bronze of her own. She eventually got tired of being known as "Nadia's best friend," retired from gymnastics, and joined the Troupe Cornea traveling circus.

Famed clown Emmett Kelly portrayed himself in the Academy Award–winning film *The Greatest Show on Earth*. However, he wasn't completely happy with the finished film because in one shot he is seen without his trademark makeup.

The Flying Wallendas were famous for performing their act without a safety net. This led to tragic consequences in Detroit in 1962, when their 7-person pyramid collapsed on the high wire, causing 3 performers to plummet 30 feet onto a concrete floor.

There were seven Ringling Brothers total, but only five of them were involved with the circus: Al, Otto, Alf, Charles, and John.

In 1999, 22-year-old Johnathan Lee Iverson became the youngest ringmaster in the history of the Ringling Brothers and Barnum and Bailey Circus. He was also the first African American to hold the position.

College Sports Champs

If you want to root college sports teams to national championships, California is the place you ought to be. Three Golden State universities—Stanford, UCLA, and USC—have each (by a wide margin) won more NCAA national titles than any other American school.

Only once in history—when Minnesota went 8–2 in 1960—has an NCAA Division I football champion lost more than one game. The Golden

Gophers were voted #1 even though another team, the Ole Miss Rebels, went undefeated that season with 11 wins and 1 tie.

Over the last 40 years, NCAA Division I wrestling has been dominated by only five select universities: Iowa, Iowa State, Minnesota, Oklahoma, and Oklahoma State. In fact, those teams have won almost every national championship since 1968, save for Arizona State's victory in 1988.

While the location of the Division I championship event for most sports changes venues each year, it remains the same for baseball. Since 1950, the College World Series has been held in the friendly confines of "The Blatt," Johnny Rosenblatt Stadium in Omaha, Nebraska.

Ten times during the 50 years from 1947–1997, a consensus national champion college football team couldn't be chosen, so the Bowl Championship Series was initiated in 1998 to correct this problem. It didn't help, as only five years later, the AP voted Southern California number one even though they didn't participate in the "national championship game."

No team has ever dominated college basketball like UCLA. In the span from 1964 to 1976, the Bruins won 10 national championships, including a run of seven in a row, and placed third twice.

Colors

After some tough talk from the lawyers at Kraft Foods, punk-metal band Green Jellö (who hit the charts in 1993 with a bizarre version of "Three Little Pigs") was forced to change its name to Green Jellÿ.

The official colors of the New York Mets baseball team are Dodger Blue and Giant Orange, in honor of the two National League teams that moved out of the city in 1957 and 1958.

Beginning in the mid-1950s, Hershey attempted to find a share of the candy-coated chocolate market by offering bags of Hershey-ets. But while their key competition (M&M's) used multiple coating colors, Hershey-ets were only made in brown.

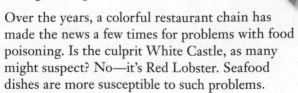

In the United States, the first widespread use of colorful ribbons to honor a cause occurred in 1979 when millions of Americans displayed yellow ribbons in support of the American hostages being held in Iran.

Over the years, a colorful restaurant chain has made the news a few times for problems with food poisoning. Is the culprit White Castle, as many might suspect? No—it's Red Lobster. Seafood dishes are more susceptible to such problems.

In Carlo Collodi's original version of *Pinocchio*, no "Blue Fairy" character appeared to rescue the youngster, and the boy formerly made of wood was actually hanged for his mischief at the end of the story.

Columnists

Do you ever wonder what the difference is between "excuse me" and "pardon me"? According to syndicated etiquette columnist Miss Manners, you should say "excuse me" when you cause inconvenience to someone and "pardon me" to let someone know they've caused inconvenience to you.

When humor columnist Erma Bombeck and her family were based in Centerville, Ohio, her neighbor and good friend was future talk show host Phil Donahue.

Before finding fame as a sports columnist, Mitch Albom worked as an amateur boxer, nightclub singer, pianist, and stand-up comic.

Hollywood gossip columnist Walter Winchell was the first person to break the news that Lucille Ball was expecting a "blessed event" in 1952. He was acknowledged on an episode of *I Love Lucy* in the song "We're Having a Baby (My Baby and Me)" with the lyric, "You'll read it in Winchell; we're adding a limb to our family tree."

The late Ann Landers, known as Eppie Lederer to her friends, was married to Jules Lederer, who founded Budget Rent-A-Car in 1958. The couple's only child, Margo Howard, wrote *Slate* magazine's "Dear Prudence" advice column for eight years.

Acid-tongued Hollywood gossip maven Hedda Hopper threatened to "out" several stars she suspected of being gay during her career, despite the fact that her own son, *Perry Mason* co-star William Hopper, was homosexual.

Before Dave Barry found his niche as a humor columnist, he worked for a consulting firm teaching effective writing to business people. He has since described it as eight years of trying to get his students to stop writing things like "Enclosed please find the enclosed enclosures."

Condiments

One of the four areas of taste on our tongue is salt, which has been used as a food preservative since prerefrigeration days. Scientists have also determined that the human body requires at least 3 grams of salt per day for things like proper temperature regulation, so we've developed a certain craving for salt as a matter of evolution.

Black pepper is indigenous to India but found its way to Rome in the first century B.C.E. Prior to that time, much of the available food was on the bland side, so a sprinkle of pepper gave otherwise plain fare a new zest. A heavier dose of pepper helped to camouflage the taste of spoiled food, which was a common problem in warm climates.

Ketchup originated in Asia as a pickled fish sauce called "ke-tsiap" and was comprised of anchovies, mushrooms, walnuts, and kidney beans. When

British seamen brought the stuff home with them, they Anglicized the name first to "catchup" and then "ketchup." When the recipe made its way across the Atlantic in the late 1700s, New Englanders added tomatoes to the mix.

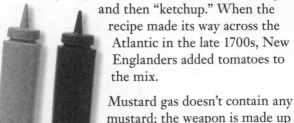

Mustard gas doesn't contain any mustard; the weapon is made up of chemicals that give it a mustardy smell and a brownish-yellow color, which is how it got its name.

When Best Foods bought the Hellman's brand in 1932, the latter already had solid name recognition in the eastern states. As a result, today the company's mayonnaise west of the Rockies is labeled *Best Foods*, while east of that area, it's still known as *Hellman's*.

Edmund McIlhenny originally packaged his famous Tabasco Hot Pepper Sauce in old cologne bottles capped with sprinkler-type fittings. The sauce was so hot (for that time) that he wanted to make sure folks sprinkled small amounts of it on their food, rather than pouring it on.

In 1981, the USDA tried to have ketchup and pickle relish classified as vegetables for their subsidized school lunch programs. Public outcry shot down the idea, but in 1998, the USDA decreed that schools could count salsa as one of their required vegetable servings.

Contests

In 2001, a Hooters waitress sued the restaurant chain after she won a company sales contest. The promised prize had been described as a Toyota, but when she was led blindfolded out into the parking lot to collect her prize, it turned out to be a "Toy Yoda"—a *Star Wars* action figure.

During the 1950s, the majority of contests were "jingle-based"—companies inviting consumers to create rhyming advertisements for their products. Evelyn Ryan of Defiance, Ohio, had such a knack for verse that she managed to keep her family home from foreclosure and keep her 10 children fed and clothed via her contest winnings. She was even the subject of the 2005 film *The Prize Winner of Defiance, Ohio*.

The Canadian Competition Act bans all games of chance, with the exception of provincial lotteries and those held at licensed casinos. As a result, most U.S.-based sweepstakes mention in the fine print that "Canadian residents will be required to answer a skill-testing question."

After winning the Nathan's Hot Dog Eating Contest six years in a row, Takeru Kobayashi was finally defeated in 2007. The younger and larger Joey Chestnut won the July 4 event by downing a world-record 66 franks (with buns) in 12 minutes.

In 1984, MTV sponsored a contest in conjunction with John Mellencamp's hit song "Pink Houses"—the grand prize being a little pink house in Bloomington, Indiana. Susan Miles of Bellevue, Washington, was ultimately awarded the deed. She spent two nights in the house, held on to the title long enough to get a tax credit, and then sold it.

McDonald's first offered a Monopoly collect-and-win stamp game in 1987 and has continued it annually since 1991. While a scandal involving prizes later caused quite a ruckus, some "real people" did win larger prizes, including one of the authors of this book, who nabbed a $2,000 prize in the mid-1990s.

Counties

According to the U.S. Census Bureau, Kalawao County, Hawaii, is not only the smallest U.S. county geographically, with only 13 square miles of land, but also the second-smallest in population, with fewer than 150 residents. It's the home of the Kalaupapa settlement, where Father Damien famously operated a leper colony on the north side of Molokai Island.

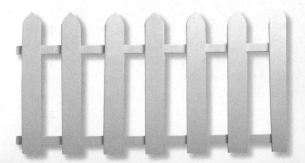

In 2005, King County, Washington, officially changed its name—*without* changing it. Originally named for former vice president William Rufus King, the state approved the county's new namesake: Dr. Martin Luther King Jr.

Of the states that are divided into counties, Delaware has the fewest, with only three. Alaska is split up into *boroughs* and outlying *census areas*, while Louisiana is comprised of *parishes*.

Each of New York City's five boroughs is also its own county: The Bronx is in Bronx County, Brooklyn is in Kings County, Manhattan is in New York County, Queens is in Queens County, and Staten Island is in Richmond County.

The 6 million people living in Dallas, Texas, are spread out over 5 different counties: Collin, Denton, Kaufman, Rockwall, and Dallas, of which Dallas is the county seat.

California's Los Angeles County is (by a 2–1 margin) the most populous county in the United States, with more than 10 million residents. Second is Cook County, Illinois, with just over 5 million, and Harris County, Texas, with nearly 4 million.

Currencies of the World

Neither two-cent coins nor two-dollar bills have enjoyed success in the United States, but they're widely used elsewhere in the world. The Euro currency used throughout much of Europe includes a 2-cent coin, a 20-cent coin, a €2 bill, and a €200 bill.

Linguists aren't certain how the name "quid" began being used in the United Kingdom as a slang term for their main unit of currency, the *pound*. Some sources say it refers to the Latin term for "what," to which we say: what?

Depending on the destination, an American traveling abroad may be better off using U.S. cash instead of exchanging it for the local currency. Some merchants may offer better exchange rates than the banks to get their hands on American cash because it tends to hold its value better than any other nation's money.

In fact, not every foreign nation has its own money. After struggling with triple-digit inflation rates, in 2000 the country of Ecuador decided to change its official national currency from the *sucre* to the U.S. dollar.

Have you ever wondered why certain foreign coins, particularly those in Asia and Africa, are minted with holes in the middle? No, it's not to save precious metal. It's so that the coins can be strung together, which is still a common practice in some areas of the world.

Banknotes made in Mexico since 2006 are imprinted with special raised designs that allow the visually impaired to distinguish the value of the bills.

Dairy Products

Buttermilk was once a by-product of churning butter (it was the liquid runoff), but today it's made by adding a lactic acid bacteria culture to skim or nonfat milk.

Dr. Elie Metchnikoff, a Russian scientist and Nobel laureate, was the first to write about the intestinal tract health benefits of eating yogurt, back in 1908. The active culture found in yogurt was named *Lactobacillus bulgaricus* in honor of Dr. Metchnikoff's work and his studies of the long-lived, yogurt-eating Bulgarians.

Despite its name, sour cream has a limited shelf life and can go bad. Unopened, it is usually still edible three weeks beyond the "sell by" date.

Clotted cream doesn't sound particularly appetizing, but it's a British delicacy. It is a pasteurized heavy cream that has the consistency of softened butter and is heavenly when spread on a warm scone.

Shelf space is limited in the dairy aisle of supermarkets, so eggnog lovers have a hard time finding it year round. American consumers associate eggnog with Thanksgiving and Christmas, so once January 1 rolls around, eggnog is banished to make room for steady sellers, such as cottage cheese and chip dip.

Turkey eggs are just as edible as chicken eggs, but they're not nearly as cost-efficient for farmers. Chickens start laying at 19 weeks, while turkeys hold off until 32 weeks. Due to their size, turkeys also require much more nesting room than chickens.

Desserts

When Boston Cream Pie was first invented, Colonial Americans didn't have deep cake pans. So when constructing the confection that eventually became known as Boston Cream Pie, bakers prepared the two sponge cake layers in pie tins.

In 1894, Georges Auguste Escoffier, the chef at London's Savoy Hotel, combined peaches, vanilla ice cream, and raspberry puree and dubbed it "Peach Melba" in honor of the Australian opera star Nellie Melba.

In New Orleans in 1951, Chef Paul Blangé of Brennan's restaurant created "Bananas Foster" as a way to promote the many tons of bananas shipped daily into the Louisiana port city from South America.

The main difference between devil's food cake and plain old chocolate cake is baking soda. When baking soda is added to the batter, it reacts with the natural acidity of the cocoa to produce the telltale slight reddish tint found in traditional devil's food.

In the early 1900s, immigrants arriving at Ellis Island were given a dish of Jell-O gelatin as a "Welcome to America" snack.

McDonald's bowed to public pressure and replaced their fried apple and cherry pies with a healthier baked version in 1992. However, nostalgic pie fans can still find the fried variety at some smaller McDonald's outlets that don't have enough room for the oven necessary to bake the pies.

Diamonds

The diamond mining industry in South Africa began in 1866, when Stephanus Erasmus Jacobs found an unusual pebble on the south bank of the Orange River. He gave it to a friend, who gave it to a friend, and so on, until it finally ended up in the hands of a professional, who determined that the "pebble" was a 21¼-carat diamond.

Princess Margaret of England once commented on Elizabeth Taylor's 39-carat Krupp diamond, calling it the most vulgar thing she'd ever seen. When Liz let the Princess try the ring on, she noticed Margaret admiring it in the light and said, "See? It's not so vulgar now, is it?"

In 1947, DeBeers hired the N.W. Ayer advertising agency to come up with a campaign that would encourage Americans to buy more expensive diamonds and hang on to them, instead of pawning or reselling them. The result was the "A diamond is forever" slogan.

Hawaii's Diamond Head got its name in the late 1700s when western traders found what they thought were diamonds on the crater. The stones they'd found, however, turned out to be calcite crystals, not valuable gemstones.

A chemically pure diamond has no color and is clear. Impure diamonds tend to have a yellowish or brownish hue. So-called natural "fancy color" diamonds occur when trace elements in the stone are irradiated during the gem's creation.

Only about 20 percent of the world's diamond supply is used for jewelry. Diamonds are also used in industry for cutting, grinding, and polishing everything from eyeglasses to the drums in copying machines to automobile pistons.

Diana, Princess of Wales

Diana felt like a disappointment for much of her younger life and often thought that she wouldn't have been born had her older brother not died when he was only 11 hours old. Her parents already had two daughters, and they were hoping for a male heir when Diana was born in 1961.

Diana stopped speaking to her former sister-in-law, Sarah Ferguson, the Duchess of York, after Fergie revealed that she'd contracted plantar warts after wearing some of Diana's old shoes.

She was "the People's Princess" in more ways than one: Diana appeared on the cover of *People* magazine a record 52 times, more than any other subject.

The Princess was known to be very generous to friends and acquaintances. When BBC reporter Jennie Bond complimented Diana on the lustrous sheen of her pantyhose, Diana had six pairs of the stockings gift-wrapped and sent to the reporter later that day.

Even though Diana reportedly enjoyed her turn on the dance floor with John Travolta at a White House dinner in 1985, the man she secretly longed to dance with that evening was ballet star Mikhail Baryshnikov, whom she had admired since she was a young girl.

According to her butler, the true love of Diana's life was not Dodi Fayed, but a heart surgeon named Hasnat Khan. Her code name for him was DDG— Drop Dead Gorgeous.

Disaster Films

Disaster movies aren't for youngsters, but that didn't stop the MPAA from giving 1970's *Airport* a "G" rating, something not shared by any of the genre films that followed it.

You may never have noticed, but in the classic 1972 disaster film *The Poseidon Adventure*, the camera rocks slowly back-and-forth during every scene in the movie to mimic the motion of the sea.

The Day After was a graphic depiction of a nuclear holocaust. Even though it was the highest-rated made-for-TV movie of all time, pulling 100 million viewers, it was only the third most-watched TV telecast in 1983, behind *Super Bowl XVII* and the final episode of *M*A*S*H*.

Among the cast of the 1974 thriller *The Towering Inferno*, you'll see the name of a 27-year-old athlete who was just beginning his feature film career at the time: Orenthal James (O. J.) Simpson.

1998's *Armageddon*, about an asteroid on a collision course with Earth, was a family affair—at least for the Tylers. While young Liv Tyler starred as Grace Stamper in the film itself, her father Steven sang lead vocals on four Aerosmith tunes on the movie's soundtrack.

With taglines like, "It's more than a speculation; it's a prediction," *The Swarm* invaded the United States in 1978. While their fears would prove false, the film convinced gullible Americans that killer bees would begin spreading throughout the United States sometime during the early 1980s.

Disco

Ever wonder how John Travolta kept his shirt from coming untucked during his frenetic dance scenes in *Saturday Night Fever*? It was specially designed so that it buttoned at the crotch.

Bernard Edwards and Nile Rodgers of Chic had a few hits to their credit, but they were still refused entrance to New York's legendary Studio 54 on 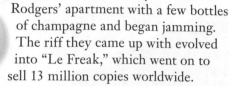 New Year's Eve 1977. They returned to Rodgers' apartment with a few bottles of champagne and began jamming. The riff they came up with evolved into "Le Freak," which went on to sell 13 million copies worldwide.

Earlier records had *sold* a million copies, but Johnnie Taylor's number one hit, "Disco Lady," was the first single to be awarded a platinum single by the RIAA. Why is that? The funky song was the first to sell a million copies *after* the RIAA first introduced the award in 1977.

Victor Willis, the original police officer and lead singer of the Village People, didn't always stay at the YMCA. He was once married to Phylicia Rashad, who portrayed mother Clair Huxtable on TV's *The Cosby Show*.

On July 12, 1979, the White Sox were forced to forfeit to the Tigers when Chicago DJ Steve Dahl's "Disco Demolition Night" promotion went awry. The previous night's game had attracted 15,000 fans, so stadium officials were unprepared for the 90,000 who showed up and swarmed the field between games.

Record producer Tom Moulton was the brainchild behind extended remixes for disco songs, created so that folks could fully enjoy dancing to a song for more than three minutes. He came up with the concept of the 12-inch single, the first of which was Moment of Truth's "So Much for Love."

Dolls and Action Figures

Johnny Gruelle, the man behind the Raggedy Ann doll, became a vocal antivaccination activist after his daughter Marcella died from what he claimed was a reaction to a smallpox vaccine she received. He even used the doll in posters promoting his stance.

The British version of G. I. Joe is called Action Man.

In 1976, Ideal Toys released a Joey Stivic doll, sold under the name "Archie Bunker's Grandson." It was the first anatomically correct male doll sold in the United States.

Mattel recalled their Cabbage Patch Snacktime Kids dolls in January 1997 after it was discovered that in addition to the supplied plastic food, the dolls also gobbled up the long hair of their "mommies" and didn't stop until they reached the scalp.

The first Ken dolls, introduced two years after Barbie hit the market, had a fuzzy, glue-on crew cut. Unfortunately, the hair rubbed off easily, and Ken's male-pattern baldness made Barbie look like she was dating her father.

In 1999, Mattel launched *Rad* Repeatin' Tarzan, a doll with a spring-loaded arm that waved up and down when Tarzan yodeled his trademark yell. However, when Tarzan was still encased in his restrictive box on toy store shelves, his arm moved up and down over his loincloth region only, and enough parental complaints eventually got the doll recalled and revamped.

Drug Stores and Pharmacies

Most drug stores keep cold and sinus medications behind the counter these days in an effort to prevent the production of illegal methamphetamine. But Oregon was the first state to enact a bill that requires a doctor's prescription for any product containing pseudoephedrine.

There is a sign at the South Pole that plugs the famous apothecary/tourist attraction, Wall Drug, South Dakota. The sign reads "Free Ice Water, 9,333 miles."

Drug stores didn't become self-serve (with products out on shelves for customers to browse through and select) until after 1920. In most stores, the pharmacist was also the proprietor, and he needed to keep an eye out for shoplifters as well as fill prescriptions. That's why pharmacists started working on raised platforms.

When Charles Walgreen first arrived in Chicago in 1893, he tossed what little money he had into the Chicago River. He reasoned that this would force him to commit himself to working hard in order to succeed.

The Rx symbol used to represent a prescription is actually a capital letter R with a line through its leg. It is the symbol for the Latin word "recipe," which translates to "take thou."

In the United Kingdom, if you hope to find a drug store or *chemist*, as it's called there, you'd be smart to keep an eye out for a sign that says "Boots." No, that doesn't mean you can find sinus medicine and footwear at the same store; Boots is the name of Britain's leading drug store chain.

Educational Terms

The word *sophomore* is based on a combination of Greek words that translates to "wise fool." The term was first used in the academic sense to describe students at Cambridge University when it opened in the sixteenth century.

In the days when folks still spoke Latin, a *baccalarius* was "a junior member of the guild." Over the years, the spelling of the word changed, as did the meaning: an apprentice student or tradesman, someone who had passed a basic level of training. And that's why today we call a four-year diploma a "Bachelor's degree."

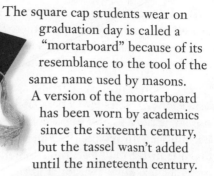

The square cap students wear on graduation day is called a "mortarboard" because of its resemblance to the tool of the same name used by masons. A version of the mortarboard has been worn by academics since the sixteenth century, but the tassel wasn't added until the nineteenth century.

Since 1970, a three-year degree from an accredited law school has been called a "Juris Doctor" or J.D. in the United States, replacing the LL.B. (Bachelor of Law) degree issued up to that time. It's the same education, same amount of study; only the names have been changed to protect the pompous.

The very first university degrees were licenses to teach. As part of the graduation process, the student delivered his first lecture as an officially licensed teacher. This ceremony was called "commencement" because it represented a beginning—the graduate could now "commence to teach."

Why is a diploma referred to as a "sheepskin"? Until the art of papermaking was fine-tuned, diplomas were handwritten on thin sheets of sheep flesh.

Elephants

Cecile de Brunhoff was a French pianist who in 1930 made up a story about an orphaned elephant to tell her sons at bedtime. Her husband fashioned her tale into a children's picture book, *Bebe Elephant*, which eventually was published as *The Story of Babar*.

Circus impresario P. T. Barnum was a trustee and benefactor of Tufts University. When Barnum's star attraction, Jumbo the Elephant, passed away, Barnum had his hide stuffed and presented him to Tufts in 1889. The school adopted the beloved pachyderm as their mascot, and their athletic teams are known as the Jumbos.

Elephants use their trunks to beat on the ground to determine whether it's safe to walk on. If they determine the path is sturdy, they will proceed by placing their rear feet in the exact same footprints created by the front feet.

Smedley the Elephant became the mascot for Cap'n Crunch's then-new Peanut Butter Crunch cereal in 1969. Smedley has since gone the way of other discarded Crunch mascots, including the Crunchberry Beast and Harry S. Hippo, the purveyor of Punch Flavored Crunch.

African elephants have larger ears than their Asian cousins. They also have two "fingers" at the tips of their trunks, whereas Asian elephants have only one.

Just like dolphins, parrots, and bats, elephants imitate and vocalize sounds from their environment. Researchers have noted that elephants growing up in zoos and rescue sanctuaries often imitate the sounds of not only other species of animals but also traffic noises.

E-Mail

While at least three providers claim to provide more e-mail accounts globally than any other, sources reveal that Yahoo! and its 200 million e-mail addresses are tops in that department.

The earliest documented mass junk e-mail, or spam, dates back to May 1978. A marketing rep for Digital Equipment Corporation, which was later bought by Hewlett-Packard, sent it. DEC prepared a message about an upcoming event to promote their new DEC-20 computer and sent it out to several hundred unsuspecting people.

Ray Tomlinson not only sent the very first e-mail message back in 1971, but he is also the person who came up with the concept of the @ sign for e-mail addresses.

The Nigerian Advance Fee Fraud scam was conducted via snail mail and telex before e-mail became common. It is often referred to simply as the "419 scam" in reference to the article of the Nigerian criminal code it violates.

President Bill Clinton only sent two e-mails while in office: one was a test message, and the other was to Sen. John Glenn when he was orbiting the earth in the space shuttle Discovery in 1998.

Even if you haven't heard of Elwood Edwards, you've probably heard him. His is the voice that announces "Welcome," "You've got mail," and "Goodbye" for America Online.

Emmy Awards

Beginning in 1985, John Larroquette won four consecutive Best Supporting Actor Emmy Awards for his role as sleazy Dan Fielding on *Night Court*. He asked that his name be removed from the ballot in 1989 to give someone else a chance.

Edward Asner has won five Emmy Awards for the same character, but on two different series. He won three statues for his role as Mary's feisty boss Lou Grant on *The Mary Tyler Moore Show* and two for the crusty newspaper editor Lou Grant on the drama series of the same name.

When it was announced that Alan Alda had won the Emmy for Best Writing in a Comedy Series at the 1979 awards show (for the *M*A*S*H* episode entitled "Inga"), Alda expressed his joy by doing a cartwheel in the aisle on his way up to accept the award.

The original name for the award was the "Immy," shorthand for *image orthicon tube*, an integral component of early TV cameras. The Academy decided that "Emmy" better suited the very feminine statuette.

Powers Boothe accepted his Best Actor award in person when he won an Emmy for his role in *Guyana Tragedy: The Story of Jim Jones.* The Writer's Guild was embroiled in a strike at the time and boycotted the awards ceremony—Boothe was the only nominated performer who showed up to claim his award.

Even though the Academy Awards are all about movies, the television broadcast of the Oscar ceremonies has won many Emmy Awards over the years, for everything from Best Choreography to Best Costumes to Best Variety Special.

End-Zone Dances

Instead of handing the football to the ref, Tommy McDonald of the Philadelphia Eagles heaved it into the stands after making a touchdown one Sunday afternoon in 1960. Sports historians refer to that gesture as the first "post-touchdown celebration."

In 1965, wide receiver Homer Jones of the New York Giants pounded the ball at the ground after a TD—the first reported "spike." Eight years later, Isaac Curtis of the Cincinnati Bengals put a new spin on the spike when he tossed the ball backward over his shoulder after crossing the goal line.

Elmo Wright took the celebration to a new level in 1973 when he punctuated his touchdown with a high-stepping, running-in-place interlude before spiking the ball. The next season, Billy "White Shoes" Johnson turned the end zone into a cabaret as he performed his own version of the Funky Chicken after scoring.

In 2003, wide receiver Joe Horn of the New Orleans Saints was fined $30,000 after an end-zone call to his mother during a game against the Giants. How did he pull off this over-the-top celebration? After he scored a touchdown, a teammate handed him a cell phone that had been concealed in the padding around the goal post.

It was the Washington Redskins and the collective high-five performed by their "Fun Bunch" that finally made the NFL clamp down on excessive end-zone celebrations after the 1984 season.

U.S. Secretary of State Condoleezza Rice is a lifelong football fan. Her favorite touchdown celebration? The Ickey Shuffle, popularized by running back Elbert "Ickey" Woods of the Cincinnati Bengals.

Eponymous Diseases

New York physician George Huntington was only 22 years old in 1872 when he published a paper describing the condition that caused involuntary twitches and tremors now known as Huntington's Chorea. He also correctly surmised at the time that the disease was hereditary and never skipped a generation.

Alois Alzheimer was a German doctor who would eventually gain fame after studying an otherwise healthy 51-year-old female patient who was showing signs of dementia. After her death, he autopsied her brain and noted abnormalities in the cerebral cortex.

For hundreds of years, leprosy was thought to be a hereditary disease or a curse from God. In 1873, Dr. Gerhard Henrik Armauer Hansen of Norway discovered the bacterium that causes leprosy, and the condition is now more properly referred to as Hansen's Disease.

James Parkinson was a British physician who wrote some of the first medical papers describing gout and the connection between an inflamed appendix and peritonitis. But he will always be remembered for his 1817 essay on the "Shaking Palsy" which today is known as Parkinson's Disease.

Until 1961, the condition known as Down Syndrome was commonly referred to as "Mongolian Idiocy." The World Health Organization voted to change the name to honor John Langdon Down, the physician who first described the characteristic head shape and hand folds of children born with the syndrome.

When campaigning for the presidency, John F. Kennedy went to great lengths to project an image of youth and vigor in order to hide the fact that he was suffering from Addison's Disease. Various photos of Kennedy during that era show the facial puffiness that resulted from the heavy doses of steroids he was taking.

Executions

Sterilizing the arm prior to administering a lethal injection may seem odd, but there is always the chance of a last-minute stay of execution. Officials want to take all necessary precautions to prevent infection "just in case."

Currently, 38 of the 50 states sanction capital punishment. However, a person who commits a federal crime in a state that bans the death penalty can still face the possibility of execution.

Saddam Hussein's last meal, per his request, was boiled chicken and rice. Along with that, he drank several cups of hot water mixed with honey, a childhood favorite of his.

In 1846, the state of Michigan became the first English-speaking government entity in the world to ban the death penalty.

Ruth Snyder wasn't the first woman to die in the electric chair, but she was one of the most memorable, thanks to a photograph on the front page of *The New York Daily News*. Thomas Howard had smuggled a tiny camera into the viewing area and snapped a picture at the moment Snyder was executed.

The Manson Family members who participated in the Tate-LaBianca murders were all sentenced to death. However, in 1972, California declared the death penalty to be unconstitutional, so their sentences were commuted to life in prison. As a result, all of them are currently eligible for parole.

Gary Gilmore signed an organ donor card while on Death Row. Within hours of his execution by firing squad, two patients received his corneas.

Eyes

Sammy Davis Jr., Sandy Duncan, and Peter Falk all had or have one glass eye. Davis lost an eye in an automobile accident, while Duncan and Falk had theirs removed due to cancer.

Prior to the discovery of anesthetic eye drops in 1884, cataract surgery was performed under general anesthesia, which made it all the more risky. Interestingly enough, the active ingredient in those first numbing eye drops was cocaine.

In 1962, David Bowie got into a schoolyard fight over a girl. A punch in the eye from George Underwood resulted in a paralyzed pupil for Bowie, which is why the singer's eyes appear to be two different colors.

If the white of your eye can be seen over the top and bottom of your iris, the colored part of your eye, your doctor will immediately suspect thyroid problems. The excess hormones produced cause the tissue behind the eye to swell, which causes the eyeball to protrude.

Your eyes are set back further in your head than your forehead or your cheeks so that if you receive a blow to the eye, your brow and cheekbone will take the brunt of the impact.

Allan Pinkerton opened the Pinkerton National Detective Agency in Chicago in 1850. He and his employees specialized in covert, undercover work, and the company's logo, an unblinking eye with the motto "We Never Sleep," inspired the term "private eye."

Familiar Tunes

The first recorded occurrence of the melody that we now sing as "Shave and a Haircut, Two Bits" is in an 1899 song by Charles Hale, called "At a Darktown Cakewalk." In 1914, Jimmie Monaco and Joe McCarthy released a song called "Bum-Diddle-De-Um-Bum, That's It!" utilizing those familiar seven notes.

"Chopsticks" was published in London in 1877 under the name "The Celebrated Chop Waltz." A 16-year-old girl named Euphemia Allen wrote the song, which has nothing to do with Chinese eating utensils. The song was intended to be played by "chopping" at the keys with the pinky fingers of both hands.

That pipe organ theme we associate with circus clowns is actually called "Entrance of the Gladiators" and was written in 1897 by the Czech composer Julius Fučík.

"Hava Nagila" started out as a wordless tune that was hummed by the Hasidim of Sadigora in what is now the Ukraine. At the turn of the twentieth century, a Latvian cantor wrote lyrics to the tune, based on text found in Psalm 118:24.

Werner Thomas is the man behind the infamous Chicken Dance. A Swiss accordionist and restaurateur, Thomas wrote a tune called "Der Ententanz" ("The Duck Dance") in his spare time after watching the ducks and geese that gathered outside his diner.

Many restaurants have their own personalized "Happy Birthday" song that they sing to customers in order to save money. The lyrics to "Happy Birthday to You" are copyrighted, and any public performance would require a royalty payment.

Famous Fires

On July 6, 1944, the tent of the Ringling Brothers and Barnum and Bailey circus caught fire during the matinee performance. Unfortunately, the canvas had been waterproofed with a mixture of gasoline and paraffin, which caused the flames to spread in record time.

When fire broke out at Our Lady of the Angels school in Chicago in 1959, there were no alarms in the building connected to the fire department, no fire-resistant stairwells, and no sprinkler system. The one positive that came out of the tragedy was the nationwide change in school fire safety regulations.

When Boston's Cocoanut Grove nightclub went up in flames in 1942, one of the leading causes of death was panicky patrons ignoring the emergency exits and trying to flee via the revolving door through which they'd entered earlier.

The Triangle Shirtwaist factory fire in New York City in 1911 resulted in several significant changes in safety laws for factories. Most importantly: all exit doors must open outward and remain unlocked during working hours (two factors that caused a majority of the Triangle deaths).

During a 1913 Christmas party held on the second floor of the Italian Hall in Calumet, Michigan, some unknown person shouted "Fire!" The resulting panic claimed the lives of 73 people and led to a Supreme Court decision regarding free speech and Oliver Wendell Holmes' famous "shouting fire in a crowded theater" ruling.

When fire broke out at Chicago's Iroquois Theater on December 30, 1903, vaudeville great Eddie Foy Jr. ordered the asbestos curtain to be lowered and stayed onstage for much of the ordeal trying to keep the crowd calm.

Fathers

British children have their own version of Santa Claus. Called Father Christmas in the United Kingdom, he traditionally wore a green hooded cloak. But as American culture slowly worked its way across the Atlantic in the 1930s, Father Christmas started wearing the traditional red fur coat associated with the iconic American Santa Claus.

Thirteen-year-old Charles Manson was sent to Father Flanagan's Boys Town in 1947. Within a week of arriving, he and another boy escaped and committed two armed robberies.

According to the American Retail Association, Americans spend about $2 billion less on gifts for Dad on Father's Day than they do for Mom on Mother's Day. Dad does place at the top in one category, however; according to AT&T, more collect calls are placed on Father's Day than any other day of the year.

The hymn "Eternal Father" is known in the United States as "The Navy Hymn" because it has been sung at each Sunday's Divine Services in Annapolis since 1879. It was

Franklin D. Roosevelt's favorite hymn, and the Navy Band played it as John F. Kennedy's body was carried up the stairs of the Capitol to lie in state.

Humorist Ralph Schoenstein has many books to his credit, including the *I Hate Preppies Handbook*, but one of his most popular publications doesn't even list his name on the cover. Schoenstein was the ghostwriter responsible for Bill Cosby's mega-selling book *Fatherhood*.

Some historians believe that Father Time is actually based on Cronus, the Titan god of agriculture, who carried a scythe for harvesting purposes. Perhaps it's because of this agricultural connection that Father Time is often depicted as being married to Mother Nature.

Female Rockers

"Hell Is for Children" was inspired by an article Pat Benatar read in *The New York Times* about child abuse in the United States. She still donates the royalties from the song to children's charities.

Patti Smith's only chart single, "Because the Night," was cowritten by Bruce Springsteen. The Boss had written the melody and the chorus but was prohibited from performing at the time due to legal issues. He gave the unfinished song to Smith, who wrote the verses in one night and had a top 20 hit.

Deborah Harry, who became the lead singer of Blondie, worked as a bunny at the New York Playboy Club from 1968 to 1973. You might not recognize her in photos from that era—she was a brunette at the time.

When Pretenders lead vocalist Chrissie Hynde attended Kent State University in Ohio, she sang in a short-lived band that included Devo founder Mark Mothersbaugh. She was also on campus the day of the infamous shootings in 1970.

"Joan Jett" seems like a name made up for the stage, but the leather-clad rocker born Joan Larkin changed her last name to her mother's maiden name, which happened to be "Jett," after her parents divorced.

Suzi Quatro was offered the role of Leather Tuscadero on TV's *Happy Days* after the producers saw her picture on the cover of *Rolling Stone* magazine. Quatro had been living overseas for several years and was unfamiliar with the show when she flew in for the audition.

Shortly after giving birth to her daughter, Jefferson Airplane vocalist Grace Slick jokingly told the nurse she was going to name the baby "god" with a small "g" so the child would remain humble. The nurse was apparently the gossipy type because the information appeared in the next day's *San Francisco Chronicle*. Grace's baby has always been named China, by the way.

Film Credits

Have you noticed how the closing credits seem to go on … and on … in recent films? Thank the various unions, who negotiated on-screen recognition as a way for behind-the-scenes folks to "sign" their work. This "signature" serves as a visual resumé and helps carpenters, electricians, and so on secure jobs on future movie productions.

A Foley artist is a sound effects specialist. Every sound in a film that isn't dialog or music is considered a sound effect. Interestingly enough, Jack Foley, the Universal Studios sound effects pioneer for whom the technique is named, never received an on-screen credit.

The opening credits of a movie follow a very specific format. The studio's name and logo appear first, followed by the name of the production company. The next credit lists the investor(s) who backed the film. After the money guys are listed, the director gets his first credit (usually listed as "a film by …").

Why do many films today sometimes list as many as a dozen producers? Most of them aren't actually producers; they're friends, personal assistants, or even fitness trainers of the film's stars. They get a production credit as a special "perk" of their relationship.

Sometimes an actor is billed as "special guest star" or "and also starring." This is usually a deal nego- tiated by an agent for so-called "name" stars who have small parts in films.

Some actors use three names because there is already another performer in the Screen Actors Guild Directory with their name. But others use it as a marketing tool; the longer the name, the more screen space it fills during the credits, making it stand out that much more among the other names.

First Pets

Soviet Premier Nikita Khrushchev presented Caroline Kennedy with a puppy named Pushinka in 1960. Pushinka came from very impressive parentage—her mother was Strelka, one of two dogs who had successfully been launched into space and returned safely on Sputnik 5.

Calvin Coolidge's roster of pets included a donkey, a pygmy hippopotamus, a bear cub, an antelope, and a pair of lion cubs, most of which were gifts from foreign leaders and diplomats. But of all his four-legged friends, his very favorite was a raccoon named Rebecca.

When the Hoover family moved to the White House, Herbert's son Allan brought his pet alliga- tors with them. The alligators slept in a bathtub at night but had free roam of the Executive Mansion during the day, which invited more than a few startled looks from visiting dignitaries.

Theodore Roosevelt's sons had a favorite pet: a calico Shetland pony named Algonquin. When young Archie Roosevelt was confined to his bed with the measles, his brother Quentin came up with the perfect plan to cheer him up. He quietly led Algonquin inside the White House, into the elevator, and up into Archie's second-floor bedroom.

President William Howard Taft pampered his pet cow, Pauline. When she wasn't outside grazing on the front lawn, she sought shelter in the White House garage among the president's four automobiles. Pauline earned her keep, however—she provided fresh milk for the first family.

The most pampered presidential pet was Fala, the Scottish Terrier that was Franklin Roosevelt's constant companion. He traveled with Roosevelt by train, car, and plane. The president always personally fed Fala by hand, and the pooch slept in a chair at the foot of FDR's bed.

Fish

Living in Trinidad in the late nineteenth century, British-born Lechmere Guppy decided to send samples of a new fish he'd "discovered" to the British Museum for identification. The species became popularly known as *guppies*.

Does the song title "Down by the Fishing Hole" sound familiar? Maybe if we whistled it, you'd remember—it's the name of the theme song from *The Andy Griffith Show*.

Doomed by its name, the orange roughy is actually a deep red—it only turns orange after death. The sudden popularity amongst the fish as a food item has caused overfishing in certain areas of the world, notably off the coasts of Australia and New Zealand.

Former Marillion lead singer Derek William Dick earned his nickname "Fish" from a former landlord who objected to the long periods he spent in the bath.

Believe it or not, *Cop Rock* might well have been the second most ridiculous police show of the 1990s, behind *Fish Police*. CBS pulled the animated series (which, as you might suspect, was about sea creatures in law enforcement) after only three episodes.

When you buy a can of sardines, it may include any of about 20 different species of fish widely classified as "sardines." You can be certain that the fish will be tightly packed in the can, however, because the sardine oil in which they're packed tends to be more expensive than the fish themselves.

Gas Stations

Many of the nation's gas stations of the past and present have adopted abbreviated names from their oil company owners. These include Amoco (American Oil Company), Arco (Atlantic Richfield Company), BP (British Petroleum), Conoco (Continental Oil Company), Sohio (Standard Oil of Ohio), Sunoco (Sun Oil Company), and Texaco (Texas Company).

Gas stations began adding fractional cent amounts to their fuel prices in the early twentieth century, when doing so made an impact in the price to fill up a tank. Eventually, all stations began using the nine tenths of a cent value, for the obvious reason that it makes prices appear almost one full cent per gallon *lower* than they actually are.

As of 2007, only two states—Oregon and New Jersey—ban self-service gas stations.

In the mid-2000s, Canadian gas stations found themselves having to replace signs nationwide after the fuel price jumped above $1 a liter, because nearly all existing signs were only set up for decimal (cent) amounts. Stations in the United States had to do the same thing back in 1979–1980, when per-gallon prices first eclipsed $1.

In 2005, the FCC formally announced there is no truth to the increasing rumors about cell phone users whose mobile devices set off fires while they were pumping gas at self-service stations. That said, the FCC recommends that you follow any precautions included in your phone's literature, as well as any signs posted by retailers curtailing cell phone use while refueling.

No, it's not your imagination; the price of gasoline does tend to rise every spring. Don't blame your local gas station though. One of the key factors influencing this is the fact that refineries undergo annual maintenance in the spring, reducing the amount of fuel available to retailers and thus raising fuel prices.

George Washington

While he's known as the Father of Our Country, George Washington wasn't a father in the more practical sense. He did adopt Martha's two children, but the couple had none of their own. (And so you know, the father of the Father of Our Country was named Augustine Washington.)

George Washington was inaugurated to his first term nearly two months late. Bad weather in March 1789 kept many congressmen from reaching the capital (which was then in New York City), so the electoral ballots couldn't be officially tallied. Washington was officially sworn in on April 30.

George Washington was the only president never to live in the White House. It wasn't built until after he left office.

How did George Washington go from being born February 11, 1741, to being born on February 22, 1742? The first was his birth date according to the Julian calendar in use at the time. But after the Gregorian calendar was implemented in 1752, adding 11 days and moving the New Year from March 21 to January 1, the date and year of his birth changed.

There were no five-star generals in the U.S. Army until World War II, so in 1976, Congress saw fit to posthumously award George Washington with a new rank, *General of the Armies of the United States*. Doing so secured his spot as the highest-ranking military officer in American history.

We tend to think of George and Martha Washington as an older couple; in fact, most of the images we see of the two depict them at an advanced age. When they married in 1759, however, both of them were only 27 years of age.

Golf

Golf club names rarely used in the game today include *baffy* (a four wood), *brassie* (a two wood), *cleek* (a two iron), *mashie* (a five iron), *niblick* (an eight iron), and *spoon* (a three wood).

Contrary to many sources, Jack Nicklaus's nickname, "The Golden Bear," has nothing to do with his blonde hair and stocky build. He earned it while playing golf in high school for the Upper Arlington (Ohio) Golden Bears.

Before good-quality synthetic materials were developed, the "carpet" at miniature golf courses was typically made from green-dyed felt made from goat hair.

In most of the world, scoring a two on a par-five hole is called an *albatross;* in the United States, it's known as a *double eagle*.

Althea Gibson was a multisport star who not only became the first African American woman to compete in tennis at Wimbledon but also the first to join the Ladies' Professional Golfing Association.

Blowing off an afternoon of work to play 18 holes is one thing—but giving up a starring role on a TV series? That's what happened when Bing Crosby was approached to play TV detective *Columbo*. He decided against the role, fearing that it would interfere with his true passion: golf. Peter Falk took the job instead.

Graffiti

The Los Angeles County Department of Public Works hired contractors to remove more than 25

million square feet of graffiti from
nearly 500,000 locations in 2005,
at a taxpayer cost exceeding $15
million.

A single drawing or inscription
on a wall, door, or other surface
is technically a *graffito*. Graffiti
is the plural form of this word
and the one most commonly
used today in both the singular
and plural contexts.

The cover of Led Zeppelin's *Physical Graffiti* album
depicts two buildings at 96/98 St. Mark's Place in
Manhattan. Those visiting the location may be
surprised to see five-story buildings because those
on the cover only had four stories. The photo was
specially cropped to "remove" one of the floors
so that the image would fit squarely on the album
cover.

Not surprisingly, statistics reveal that more than
half the graffiti that crops up in major cities is put
there by teenage boys.

Since Queen lead singer Freddie Mercury passed
away in 1991, "fans" have scrawled thousands of
items of graffiti on the brick walls in front of his
mansion in the Kensington area of London. In fact,
the walls have been pressure-cleaned so many times
that the brickwork is beginning to deteriorate.

Most laws requiring persons to be 18 years of age
to buy spray paint were initially enacted to cut
down on graffiti. Today, those same laws serve a

second purpose: to help curtail incidents of "huffing," or the purposeful inhaling of aerosols.

The cast of George Lucas's 1973 motion picture *American Graffiti* included four actors who would go on to become sitcom stars later that decade: Ron Howard (*Happy Days*), Mackenzie Phillips (*One Day at a Time*), Suzanne Somers (*Three's Company*), and Cindy Williams (*Laverne & Shirley*).

The Grand Canyon

In the middle of summer, the average high temperature on the rim of the Grand Canyon is about 80°F, but at the bottom of the gorge, you can expect daily temperatures in excess of 100°F.

The Grand Canyon is America's grandest canyon—and its largest, measuring 277 miles long—but it is not our nation's deepest. That honor goes to Hells Canyon in Idaho.

A life-size bronze statue of Brighty the burro adorns the lobby of the Grand Canyon Lodge. Made famous in a children's book by Marguerite Henry, Brighty was quite real, carrying water and giving rides to thousands of visitors in the early 1900s.

For more than 40 years, the Glen Canyon Dam has reduced the flow of the Colorado River as it runs downstream through the Grand Canyon. Environmentalists have adjusted the flow of the

dam—even creating artificial "floods" at times—
to minimize the impact of the water reduction on
the Grand Canyon ecosystem.

Grand Canyon National Park was first established
by Woodrow Wilson in 1919, but it doubled in size
in 1975 after Gerald Ford signed an act that incorporated federally owned land adjacent to the exist-
ing boundaries.

Remember when *The Flintstones* visited the Grand
Canyon, only to discover that (back then) it was
just a tiny crack in the ground made by a small
stream? Today, fans of the animated series can
see replicas of stone-age cars and even enjoy a
"Brontoburger" at Bedrock City in Valle, Arizona,
just south of the Canyon.

In March 2007, a glass walkway known as The
Skywalk opened to give visitors a view 4,000 feet
down into the canyon from above. Those brave
enough to wander out on the platform are required
to wear special shoe covers, both to prevent
slipping and to keep the glass from becoming
scratched.

The Grand Ole Opry

Ryman Auditorium was long the home of the
Grand Ole Opry, but the structure wasn't originally built for that purpose. When it opened in
1892, it was called the Union Gospel Tabernacle.
That's right—it was a church.

In 1950, a young man took the stage at the Grand Ole Opry and exhibited the banjo prowess that allowed him to win a national competition on the instrument. That 17-year-old was future *Hee-Haw* star Roy Clark.

The radio show known as *The Grand Ole Opry* began life in 1925 as the *WSM Barn Dance*. A couple years later, when announcer George "Judge" Hay described the show's music as "grand ole opry" in contrast to "grand opera," the name stuck.

Many of the most popular women ever to perform at the Grand Ole Opry aren't as recognizable by their real names. This list includes Sarah Cannon (Minnie Pearl), Christina Ciminella (Wynonna Judd), Eileen Edwards (Shania Twain), Mary Penick (Skeeter Davis), and Brenda Webb (Crystal Gayle).

Nostalgia is important in country music. When the show moved to the Opry House at Opryland in 1974, workers cut out a circular, 6-foot section of the original dark oak stage at Ryman Auditorium and installed it in the middle of the new stage floor so that new artists could perform on the same floor as legends from decades past.

Elvis Presley signed a contract to play a series of shows at the Grand Ole Opry beginning on October 2, 1954. However, management cancelled his booking after his first show because they felt his music wasn't suited for their audiences. The King never returned to the Opry stage.

Greeting Cards

Even though Nathaniel Currier and James Ives are best known for their lush Victorian Christmas scenes, they also produced significant political cartoons and banners in their lithograph shop.

Christmas still reigns supreme as the biggest card-sending holiday, but Valentine's Day runs a close second. Interestingly enough, the top recipients of Valentine cards are teachers, followed by children, mothers, and then wives.

Combine a three-volt lithium ion battery, an analog recording chip, an amplifier, and tiny speakers, and you have the workings of a musical greeting card. When the card is closed, a tab slides between the two contacts and keeps the greeting silent. Such devices draw very little juice, so a musical greeting will last much longer than your birthday party.

The very first Hallmark card, published in 1916, featured a verse from poet Edgar A. Guest: "I'd like to be the sort of friend that you have been to me."

According to the Greeting Card Association, four of every five greeting cards sold are purchased by women.

In 1848, a new Valentine's Day card tradition emerged: the "penny dreadful" or "vinegar valentine." These cards were printed on cheap stock and featured rhyming insults intended for spinsters and other lovelorn folk.

Gum

Thomas Adams came up with the idea of flavored chewing gum, but it wasn't his first thought. When exiled Mexican General Santa Anna introduced Adams to the natural latex known as *chicle* in 1869, he spent months fruitlessly trying to develop it as a substitute for more-expensive rubber in items like galoshes and bicycle tires.

Chewing gum pioneer William Wrigley started his career by selling soap to customers, offering baking powder as a free bonus. Then he switched to selling the powder and giving away free gum with each can. After the gum proved more popular than the powder, he decided to start selling the gum full time in 1892.

The earliest commercial baseball cards were included in cigarettes and other tobacco products. In the early twentieth century, when collecting cards became a juvenile passion, they were packaged with candy and, most famously, bubble gum. Today's packs include no gum at all because the residue can damage otherwise valuable cards.

Why is a 10-pack of Juicy Fruit gum on display at the Smithsonian's American History Museum? On June 26, 1974, it became the first item sold in the United States with a scan of its UPC code.

If the legend holds true, bubble gum has historically been pink because, when Walter Diemer came up with the recipe in the labs at the Fleer Company, pink was the only coloring that was readily available.

In 1944–1945, World War II rationing meant that the Wrigley Company didn't have enough ingredients to provide the American public with gum. However, they were able to produce enough to supply the military, so the company rerouted its output to the U.S. Armed Forces.

Hats

First Lady Jacqueline Kennedy wasn't a regular hat-wearer until her husband became president. When Halston designed a bone wool pillbox hat for her to wear at her husband's inauguration, she found the style so flattering that she made it her trademark.

The story of a 10-gallon hat being so named because it could hold that much water is a myth. *Galón* is the Spanish word for "braid," and back in the day, it was a tradition to have a tall-crowned hat that left room for several rows of braided hatbands. English-speaking cowboys heard "galón" and thought "gallon."

Butch Patrick (Eddie Munster) starred in an unlikely Saturday morning Krofft TV production called *Lidsville*. The show was set in a netherworld populated by oversized hat puppets, with Charles Nelson Reilly as the ringleader.

The pork-pie hat is similar to a traditional Fedora but has a flat crown. It had been traditional head-gear for British men-about-town for years, but also became popular in America thanks to silent film star Buster Keaton.

In the 1980 motion picture *The Blues Brothers*, Elwood (Dan Aykroyd) is never seen without his sunglasses, while younger brother Jake (John Belushi) never takes off his hat.

The term "hat trick" originated not with hockey, but with cricket. A bowler tricky enough to take three wickets on three consecutive balls was often rewarded by his club with a rather heady gift: a new hat. But speaking of hockey ...

Hockey

Before Frank Zamboni patented his ice-resurfacing machine in 1949, the process of preparing the ice for a hockey match took well over an hour. A tractor scraped the surface, and three or four workers followed behind, removing the ice shavings and spraying water on the surface to allow it to freeze.

Hockey great Wayne Gretzky always played with the back right side of his jersey tucked in. This tradition started when he was six years old and his jersey reached to his knees; his father tucked in the right side to facilitate his son's shooting.

Detroit hockey fans are well aware of the tradition of throwing octopi onto the ice during games. The tradition started in 1952 when the Cusimano brothers (who owned a fish stall in Eastern Market) tossed a cephalopod onto the ice during the playoffs, when eight wins were necessary to nab the Stanley Cup.

When thinking of the *Friday the 13th* slasher films, the first image that comes to many minds is that of Jason wearing a white hockey mask. However, he didn't adopt that look until he "borrowed" the mask from one of his many victims in *Friday the 13th, Part 3* (theatrically released in 3D).

Official NHL hockey pucks weigh from 5.5 to 6 ounces and are made from vulcanized rubber. They're kept in an ice-packed cooler at the officials' bench during games, because frozen pucks have less "bounce."

Over the 28 seasons from 1941–1969, three teams—the Detroit Red Wings, Montreal Canadiens, and Toronto Maple Leafs—dominated the National Hockey League. Only once in that span did one of these teams *not* take home the Stanley Cup: in 1961, when the Chicago Black Hawks emerged victorious.

I Love Lucy

Desi Arnaz, a Cuban immigrant whose first job in the United States was cleaning out birdcages at a pet store, was very loyal to his adopted country. When the writers presented him with an *I Love Lucy* script that focused on Ricky Ricardo cheating on his income tax, Desi immediately refused it.

William Frawley (Fred) was a baseball fanatic and had it written into his contract that if his favorite team, the New York Yankees, made it to the World Series, he would have paid time off to watch or attend the games. (The Yankees made the World Series six of those seven years.)

Lucy fans will notice that throughout the California episodes, the Ricardos constantly referred to their car as a Pontiac. Was this product placement? You bet. General Motors paid a hefty promotional fee to have the 1955 Star Chief Convertible featured on the nation's most popular TV show.

Of the four principal stars of the show, Desi Arnaz was the only one who was never nominated for an Emmy.

In several episodes of *I Love Lucy*, an audible "uh-oh" can be heard over the audience's laughs when a character was about to get into trouble. That voice belonged to Dede Ball, Lucille's mother, who regularly attended the filming of the show.

Desi and Lucy's children, Desi Arnaz Jr. and Lucie Arnaz, only appeared on their parents' show one time. They were briefly visible in a crowd scene during *I Love Lucy*'s final episode, "The Ricardos Dedicate a Statue."

The Ivy League

Seven of the eight Ivy League schools were founded before the American Revolution (Cornell being the exception), but the use of the term "Ivy League" to group the colleges only dates back to 1933. The seven schools are Brown, Columbia, Dartmouth, Harvard, Princeton, Yale, and the University of Pennsylvania.

According to the most recent statistics, a student has a better chance of getting into Cornell than any other Ivy League school. One in five applicants is accepted there, versus one in ten for Columbia, Harvard, and Princeton.

Most Ivy League schools require that undergraduates either exhibit an ability to swim or take a beginner's course in swimming.

While sources disagree, most historians believe that the Ivy League got its name from the spreading plants that cover many of the oldest college buildings in the American northeast. Harvard is the oldest Ivy League member and the oldest college in the United States, founded in 1636.

No Ivy League school offers athletic scholarships, which is the key reason why those universities' sports teams typically cannot compete with those from colleges that do.

The "Seven Sisters" was a septet of women's colleges considered the female equivalent to the Ivy League. Vassar became a co-ed school, and Radcliffe merged with Harvard in 1999, so the five remaining Sisters are Barnard, Bryn Mawr, Mount Holyoke, Smith, and Wellesley.

Only one state—New York—is home to two Ivy League schools: Columbia in New York City and Cornell in Ithaca.

Jingles

The Coca-Cola jingle "I'd Like to Teach the World to Sing" was reworked into a proper song and released in 1971. But it wasn't until the release of the accompanying TV commercial, featuring a crowd of young people singing the tune on a hilltop, that the jingle got any real airplay. Two versions of the song ended up hitting the Top 20.

Those cheerful voices who sing radio station IDs belong to the Johnny Mann Singers. The vocal group records jingles for stations across the country from a studio in Dallas, Texas.

That deep voice that says, "Ho, ho, ho," in the Green Giant jingle is singer Elmer "Len" Dresslar Jr. The baritone first recorded those three syllables in 1959 and continued to receive royalty checks for his effort up until his death in 2005.

In order for a sound to be trademarked, it must be inherently distinctive and unique and must also indicate to the consumer the source of the product. NBC's three-tone station-ID jingle was trademarked in 1950, the first sound to be so patented.

Ever wonder how commercial-makers got cats to "sing" the Meow Mix jingle? Ralston Purina's ad agency used some film footage of a mewing cat, which they proceeded to loop backward, forward, and backward again in order to stretch it out to 30 seconds.

Barry Manilow wrote commercial jingles to pay the bills before his recording career took off. Some of his best-known compositions include "I am stuck on Band-Aid, 'cause Band-Aid's stuck on me" and "Like a good neighbor, State Farm is there."

Labor Unions

The first labor strike in the United States occurred in 1791, when Philadelphia carpenters campaigned for 10-hour workdays and overtime pay. Despite their attempts, they were unsuccessful, and the shorter workday did not become a reality for many American workers until the Fair Labor Standards Act of 1938 enforced eight-hour workdays.

Freight haulers began organizing back in 1901 when teams of horses still transported goods in wagons. The drivers were referred to as "teamsters," which is how that union got its name.

Ronald Reagan was the only U.S. president who had previously been president of a labor union. He served as head of the Screen Actors' Guild for eight years.

"We Shall Overcome" was adapted from a gospel song written in 1900 by Charles Tindley. Union members first sang it during a 1945 strike in Charleston, South Carolina, and it quickly became the unofficial anthem of the labor movement.

Even though patrons at the now-defunct Machus Red Fox restaurant in Bloomfield Hills, Michigan, would regularly request "to sit in the booth that Jimmy Hoffa last sat in," he never made it inside for lunch that fateful day he visited. The labor leader disappeared from the parking lot on July 30, 1975, while awaiting his luncheon companion.

American labor unions are almost as old as the nation itself. As early as 1648, the seeds of unionization were planted when coopers (barrel makers) and shoemakers in Boston banded together and formed *guilds*.

Lions

Because of their fierce reputation and large manes, it's easy to assume that the male lion is truly the "king of the jungle" and the largest cat in the wild. In truth, however, that honor goes to male tigers, some of whom may exceed 750 lbs.

After winning their third league championship in six years in 1957, the Detroit Lions went on one of the coldest streaks in professional sports history. Over the next 50 seasons, this NFL team managed to win a total of *one* playoff game.

While there are several subspecies of lions, some taxonomists now believe that most (if not all) of them have a common ancestor. They believe that the changes in outward appearance among these subspecies may be due to nothing more than differing climates and diets in various parts of the world.

Disney's animated feature film *The Lion King* remains the top-selling home videotape ever released, with 30 million units sold on VHS worldwide. With the demise of the videotape format in lieu of DVD, it's a virtual certainty that this record will never be broken.

Most white lions are the result of genetic problems resulting from inbreeding while in captivity. In truth, it's more fortunate that a white lion be born in a zoo than in the African savannah because the light fur would make it difficult for a lion to capture prey without being spotted.

Bodybuilder Charles Atlas (born Angelo Siciliano) developed his "dynamic tension" exercising technique after watching the movement of the muscles of lions as they stretched their legs at Prospect Park Zoo in Brooklyn.

Malls

What do shopping malls and croquet have in common? It has to do with *pall mall*, a seventeenth-century British sport that resembled croquet (the word "mall" is based on "mallet"). When the sport waned in popularity, the open areas where it was once played became promenades. Shopkeepers sprang up on all sides, and the resulting areas became known as *malls*.

The open area in Washington, D.C., known as The Mall is situated between the Lincoln Memorial, the United States Capitol, and the Washington Monument.

Woody Allen stated in interviews that, prior to filming *Scenes from a Mall*, he'd never before set foot in a shopping mall.

Zombie fans might enjoy a visit to Monroeville Mall outside of Pittsburgh, where the 1978 horror classic *Dawn of the Dead* was filmed. If you want to roam the stores where the 2004 remake was shot, you're out of luck; Thornhill Square Mall in Ontario, Canada, was torn down shortly after the film opened.

Architect Victor Gruen is credited with designing the concept of the regional shopping center. His idea was to take established downtown department stores and bring them out to the suburbs where land was cheap and parking was plentiful. His first creation, Northland Mall in Southfield, Michigan, featured covered walkways leading to J.L. Hudson's, the "anchor" store.

Bergen Mall in Paramus is the oldest mall in New Jersey. It was also the site of teen singer Tiffany's first concert in 1987, kicking off her "mall tour."

Mark Twain

In 1835, Mark Twain was born Samuel Langhorne Clemens in Florida *and* Missouri. How is that possible? He was born in a *town* called Florida, which is located in the *state* of Missouri.

Although he was known for his decidedly American style, Mark Twain was quite the world traveler. During his lifetime, he not only journeyed all over North America and Europe but also embarked on trips to Hawaii, India, Africa, and even Australia.

Clemens was known as "Sam" while growing up and began using the pen name Mark Twain in 1863. Four years later, at the age of 31, the author published his first book, *The Celebrated Jumping Frog of Calaveras County and Other Sketches*.

Before Twain made it as a writer, his brother Orion Clemens parlayed campaign work for Abraham Lincoln into an appointment as secretary of the Nevada Territory in 1861. Sam followed to help out but, to the world's benefit, found prospecting and writing much more entertaining than government service.

Mark Twain wasn't the only famous resident of Hannibal, Missouri. Located on the banks of the Mississippi River, the town has also been home to persons real (Cliff Edwards, the voice of Jiminy Cricket), legendary (the Unsinkable Molly Brown), and fictional (Colonel Sherman Potter of TV's *M*A*S*H*).

Twain's 1863 memoir, *Life on the Mississippi*, is widely considered the first manuscript ever written on a typewriter. A few years later, Mark Twain invested heavily in an early typesetting machine that failed miserably and eventually put him into bankruptcy.

McDonald's

Before McDonald's made him a multimillionaire, Ray Kroc failed selling real estate in Florida in his 20s. Fifty years later, his wealth allowed him to purchase a huge mansion in the state. He topped it off by having electricians install a special doorbell chime that played the jingle "You Deserve a Break Today."

The Filet-O-Fish was created in 1962 by McDonald's franchiser Lou Groen, who was frustrated with losing Catholic customers to rival Big Boy, whose fish sandwiches sold very well on those days when no meat was eaten.

McDonald's Corporation founder Ray Kroc didn't think the Filet-O-Fish would be a success, so he came up with his own meatless sandwich called the Hula Burger, which was really just a slice of pineapple on a bun. The two sandwiches went head-to-head at a Chicago McDonald's on Good Friday, and the Filet became a regular menu item after winning in a landslide.

In the 2004 motion picture *Super Size Me*, a succession of women interviewed for the documentary failed to properly recite the Pledge of Allegiance, but all could remember the Big Mac ingredient jingle, which was "Two all-beef patties, special sauce, lettuce, cheese, pickles, onions on a sesame-seed bun."

Time magazine revealed that McDonald's restaurants stopped updating their "more than XX billions served" signs after they topped the 100 billion mark on April 14, 1994. Many of those signs have since been replaced with static ones reading "billions and billions served."

Dan Coudreaut became head chef at McDonald's in 2004. He's the man responsible for whittling down several hundred suggestions and ideas into a handful of potential new menu items that are introduced in the chain's restaurants around the world.

Motorcycles

In September 2006, Chris Carr became "the fastest man on two wheels" when he pushed a specially equipped motorcycle to a record speed of 350.884 mph at the wide-open Bonneville Speedway.

In 1921, Leslie "Red" Parkhurst steered a Harley-Davidson racing motorcycle to victory in several races, breaking several speed records along the way. He carried the team mascot—a pig—around the track on victory laps, a stunt that led to Harleys being commonly referred to as "Hogs."

The first working airplane engine wasn't an airplane engine at all but a motorcycle engine. The *Flyer I*, piloted by the Wright Brothers in their famous 1903 flight at Kitty Hawk, North Carolina, was powered by a 12-horsepower, chain-driven bike motor.

Accounts vary greatly as to the cause of (and severity of) Bob Dylan's famous motorcycle accident on July 29, 1966, but the event undoubtedly had a profound effect on his songwriting and his playing. Some music historians believe that he used the occurrence as an excuse to take a much-needed break from his grueling schedule.

Though their vulnerability makes them nearly useless today, armed forces made good use of motorcycles during the first half of the twentieth century. Harley-Davidson, Indian, and Triumph combined to produce more than 150,000 cycles for Allied military use during World War II, while BMW and other makers produced a smaller number of bikes for the Axis.

A national group known as ABATE, American Bikers Aimed Toward Education, have long held the stance that helmet laws should *not* be made mandatory. Their slogan is: "Let those who ride decide."

Mountains

Vermont is a combination of the French term for "green mountain," and Montana is the Spanish word for "mountainous." Idaho was at first said to be a Shoshone word meaning "gem of the mountains" but was later revealed to be a made-up name.

The notch in the oval Infiniti emblem looks like a pie that's missing a piece. In actuality, it's intended to represent the highest mountain in Japan, Mt. Fuji.

Measured from sea level, the second-tallest mountain on Earth is known by many names, but it is most commonly referred to as K2. The numeric reference has nothing to do with its height, however; it's because it was the second peak surveyed in the Karakoram Range during an 1856 European expedition.

If you head to Canada and find yourself in need of a caffeine rush, don't grab a Mountain Dew. The soft drink, known in the United States for its high caffeine content, is caffeine-free in the Great White North, where law restricts the addition of caffeine to beverages that don't naturally contain it.

In 1926, when Max Stern received 5,000 singing canaries to settle a debt owed to him, he left Germany for America. Unable to speak English, he still managed to sell the birds to Wanamaker's department store in Manhattan and used the proceeds to start his own corporate empire: the pet supply brand known as Hartz Mountain.

At 6,684 feet tall, North Carolina's Mount Mitchell is the highest peak east of the Mississippi. You don't have to go all the way to the Rockies to find a taller peak, however. In between, there's South Dakota's Mount Harney (7,242 feet) and Mount Guadalupe (8,749 feet) in Texas.

Movie Theaters

Opened in 1927, Sid Grauman's Chinese Theatre is a Tinseltown landmark, with a "who's who of celebrities" enscribed in slabs of concrete in the sidewalk out front. Less well known is the foreign-themed movie house Sid built five years prior: Grauman's Egyptian Theatre, located just down the street on Hollywood Boulevard.

The initials of the AMC theater chain stand for American Multi-Cinema. In 1963, Stanley Durwood opened the first *multiplex*, a single theatre offering movies on two or more screens, in Kansas City, Missouri. The first *megaplex* was the 24-screen AMC Grand in Dallas, opened in 1995.

An antitrust suit against Paramount led to a 1948 Supreme Court decision that forced movie studios nationwide to divest their movie theater holdings. Studios had begun keeping their popular releases away from competing theater chains, to the detriment of Hollywood. Paramount alone had to sell off its interests in nearly 1,400 theaters.

The Nickelodeon television network got its name from a term used for movie theaters of the early twentieth century; such establishments typically charged five cents—a nickel—for admission.

Were Mayan gods smiling on Colorado? Just as Denver's landmark Mayan Theatre was due for demolition in 1986, the city's Museum of Natural

History opened a new display of centuries-old Mayan artifacts from Mexico. A local group stepped in and saved the historic 1930 theatre, which underwent a $2 million facelift.

In 1953, movie theaters nationwide began to employ new tricks in an attempt to regain the audiences they had lost to television. The Cinemascope technique combined an extra-wide image with stereophonic sound, neither of which could be duplicated on TV sets of the era. (The first Cinemascope film was *The Robe*.)

Movies-Within-Movies

Some Hollywood movies include footage of fictional Hollywood films either being planned, being filmed, or being seen in a theater. Here are some of our favorites:

- *America's Sweethearts—Time Over Time*
- *An American Werewolf in London—See You Next Wednesday*
- *Austin Powers in Goldmember—Austin Powers in Austinpussy*
- *The Big Lebowski—Logjammin'*
- *Bowfinger—Chubby Rain*
- *For Your Consideration—Home for Purim*

- *Jay & Silent Bob Strike Back*—Good Will Hunting 2: Hunting Season
- *The Player*—Habeus Corpus
- *Scream 2*—Stab
- *Singin' in the Rain*—The Dueling Cavalier
- *South Park: Bigger, Longer & Uncut*—Asses of Fire
- *State and Main*—The Old Mill
- *True Romance*—Coming Home in a Body Bag, Part 2

Musical Royalty and Nobility

The band Queen was the first major act to bring rock music to South America on a grand scale. After a record-breaking tour there in 1981, the group headlined the first Rock in Rio festival four years later, playing before what at the time was the largest paying audience in history: 250,000 fans.

A struggling musician from Minnesota got the break of a lifetime when he was selected to open for the Rolling Stones in 1981, but he was booed off stage when he appeared in front of audiences wearing black panties. The young man's name? Prince.

David Bowie has played many roles and been known by many nicknames throughout his long musical career. Many still refer to him by a moniker he earned in the 1970s: "The Thin White Duke."

B. B. King's nickname wasn't always so, well, *brief*. In the late 1940s, he worked at a Memphis radio station and was known as "Riley King, the Blues Boy of Beale Street." Fans began to refer to him as "the Blues Boy," which they eventually shortened to "B. B."

The death of a princess spawned one of the top-selling singles of all time, when Elton John and collaborator Bernie Taupin revised the lyrics to "Candle in the Wind" to honor Princess Diana in 1997. The song is second only to Bing Crosby's "White Christmas" for most copies sold worldwide.

NASCAR

NASCAR owes everything to ... France? No, not the European nation, we're talking about William France Sr., who organized the National Association for Stock Car Auto Racing in Daytona, Florida, in 1948. Son Bill Jr. took the reins of the organization in 1972 before handing it over to his own son, Brian, in 2003.

Nearly every level of NASCAR competition has corporate sponsorship. The three most popular are the NEXTEL Cup (becomes Sprint Cup in 2008), the Busch Series, and the Craftsman Truck Series. The NEXTEL Cup was originally known as the Grand National Series, but became the Winston Cup after R. J. Reynolds took over sponsorship of the series in 1972.

In 1977, Cale Yarborough successfully defended his Winston Cup championship and did something en route that no driver before him had ever accomplished—he finished *every* race that season.

After NASCAR required shatterproof plastic windshields, drivers complained that they became dirty and scratched too easily during races. The solution? Clear plastic sheets are placed on the windshield that crew members can peel off one-at-a-time if they become soiled.

The NASCAR races you don't see on television or in person tend to be as dangerous as the ones you do. Three of the last four fatalities to occur in the Winston Cup/NEXTEL Cup series occurred during practice runs.

Over the last two decades (ending in 2007), Chevrolet has dominated the Daytona 500. Drivers behind the wheels of Chevys have won 15 of 20 races. During that span, the winner's purse has grown from $200,000 to a staggering $1.5 million.

National Flags

A new Iraqi flag designed in 2004 was rejected by the nation's new government before it ever hit the top of the flagpole. The design that flies above the country today is the same one that flew under Saddam Hussein's regime, including the Arabic words "God is Great" (which he added in 1991).

Three national flags aren't rectangles wider than they are tall. The flag of Nepal is an unusual five-sided banner, while the flags of Switzerland and Vatican City are perfect squares.

Look closely at the flag of Mozambique. The cross atop the open book on the left side is made by a garden hoe and a Russian-made AK assault rifle. In 1999, the government began to solicit ideas for a new flag but has rejected every one of the more than 170 proposals through 2007.

Many national flags are similar in design, but two pairs of them are indistinguishable to all but the trained eye. The red-and-white flags of Indonesia and Monaco are virtually identical, as are the blue, yellow, and red-striped flags of Chad and Romania.

Only one national flag is plain in color without any sort of design: the all-green flag of Libya.

Contrary to popular rumor, the 11 points on the maple leaf in the center of the Canadian flag do not represent "10" (the number of provinces) plus "1" (collectively for the territories). The points have no particular meanings, and on early renditions of the flag, the maple leaf was designed with more than 11 points.

National Parks

The largest national park, Wrangell-St. Elias in Alaska, is larger than nine states and covers an area of more than 13,000 square miles. In fact, Alaska is home to the next three largest National Parks in the country: Gates of the Arctic, Denali, and Katmai.

One of the nation's newest national parks is also its smallest. Wolf Trap Farm in Virginia, designated a national park in 2003, is only one fifth of a square mile in size. It's known as the first National Park for the Performing Arts.

You'll find Glacier National Park along the British Columbia border in Montana, and another Glacier National Park in British Columbia itself. The two parks aren't contiguous, however; there's about 250 miles of land between them.

At Yosemite National Park, bears that cause run-ins with visitors are usually "relocated" to remote areas of the park. Unfortunately, because bears are territorial, the tactic works only about 20 percent of the time. The creatures will often return to the easiest known source of nutrition: human food.

The first state to ratify the Constitution, Delaware, also happens to be the last state without a unit of the National Park Service. Every other state is home to 1 of 388 NPS-designated sites, including National Memorials, National Monuments, and National Historic Parks.

While Yellowstone is popularly known as the first national park, it was really the second. Congress proclaimed Arkansas's Hot Springs Reservation a "national park" back in 1832, and it was officially added to the NPS list in 1921.

The Navy

Sure, the U.S. Navy has more ships than any other branch of the U.S. military, but it's also neck-and-neck with the Air Force in terms of sky power. Both groups have more than 4,000 operational aircraft currently in service.

The U.S. Navy no longer uses the rank of commodore. It was removed shortly after World War II and briefly reintroduced from 1982–1985. The one-star rank is now known by the name rear admiral (lower half).

Like his character on *The Cosby Show*, Bill Cosby was a Navy veteran. In real life, Cosby dropped out of school in 1956 and served in the Navy as a hospital corpsman. He earned his high school diploma and, after his discharge from active duty, was awarded a track-and-field scholarship to Temple University where he became more serious about his education.

While other branches of the U.S. military train recruits at various "boot camps" across the country, the Navy only has one such facility: the Recruit Training Command center in Great Lakes, Illinois.

Navy officials gave the Village People permission to film the video for their hit single "In the Navy" aboard a destroyer, the UCS *Reasoner*. It's said that, in exchange, the Navy was given permission to use the song in their own recruiting videos. (However, they decided against doing so after viewing the finished product.)

If you hope to serve on a battleship like your great-grandfather, you're a few years too late. The use of these powerful but vulnerable ships declined after World War II, and none are currently in service for the U.S. Navy.

New York

New York City was our nation's capital from 1785–1790, both under the Articles of Confederation and the U.S. Constitution. George Washington was inaugurated as our first president in New York in 1789.

The New York subway was originally built with the intention of giving Manhattanites an easier way to get to their jobs in the outer boroughs. As more businesses moved to Manhattan and real estate there became pricey, many residents began to relocate. Today, the trains tend to carry workers to jobs on the island.

David Pace studied dentistry at Tulane, figuring that if his family's syrup business took off, he'd end up with plenty of customers. He changed gears, however, by coming up with the recipe for Pace picanté sauce. The brand became famous in the 1980s for its popular inquisitive catchphrase: "New York City?!"

A Dane working for the Dutch, Jonas Bronck became the first European to settle the land just north of Manhattan Island. The profitable farm he established led to the area being referred to as The Bronck's, which was later shortened to The Bronx.

Although Liberty Island, the land on which the Statue of Liberty stands, is part of New York, the island and the statue actually lie within the territorial waters of New Jersey.

It seems fitting that the first single off the first solo album from Bronx-born Ace Frehley of KISS would be "New York Groove." Many fans didn't know, however, that Englishman Russ Ballard wrote the song and that the band Hello had scored a European hit with it three years prior.

Longacre Square was renamed Times Square in 1904 after *The New York Times* moved its offices to a tower at Broadway and 42nd Street. Two years later, New Year's revelers first saw the big light-up "ball" drop from the sky at the now-famous spot.

Noses

If you were to stretch out Fido's nasal membrane, it would cover more space than his whole body. The average human has about 65 square inches of nasal membrane, compared to about 900 square inches for dogs. This explains why their sense of smell is so highly developed.

What item appeared as Frosty the Snowman's nose? While snowmen are often depicted with carrots as noses, Frosty's proboscis was a button, according to the song's lyrics.

Despite the fact that nose jobs have become common in Hollywood, some still feel the need to defend these surgeries with excuses other than that they're purely cosmetic. One notable example is Tori Spelling, who admitted to having the surgery in 1994, but only to repair damage caused by a nasty parrot bite.

Jimmy Durante isn't the only celebrity to make a nose print in the cement in the forecourt of Grauman's Chinese Theatre in Hollywood. Bob Hope did the same.

The Proboscis monkey, named for the large nose that hangs down towards its chins, can only be found on Borneo. The creature's diet relies on leaves and fruits from trees that don't grow anywhere but on the island.

Alfred Hitchcock joked that he would call his 1959 movie *The Man in Lincoln's Nose* (after the dramatic final chase sequence on Mt. Rushmore), but given concerns that such a name would be off-putting to moviegoers, it was changed to *North by Northwest*.

Novelty Songs and Artists

The late Bobby Pickett perfected his Boris Karloff impersonation as a youngster, and it served him well when he employed it to great effect on "Monster Mash." The song topped the music charts Halloween week in 1962 and became a perennial late-October favorite.

Best known for the novelty hits "Wooly Bully" and "Lil' Red Riding Hood," the leader of Sam the Sham and the Pharaohs wasn't named Samuel, but Domingo. The nickname was an abbreviation of his last name, Samudio.

Johnny Horton recorded two versions of his hit "The Battle of New Orleans," one for American audiences and one for release in the United Kingdom. The lyrics were changed in the overseas version to examine the historic event from the British perspective.

"Weird Al" Yankovic's second single, "Another One Rides the Bus," was recorded live on the Dr. Demento radio program in 1980. It was a step up from his first single, "My Bologna," which Al had recorded in the bathroom across the hall from the student radio station at Cal Poly.

Tom Lehrer, whose novelty hits included "The Vatican Rag" and "The Masochism Tango," was a major-league brainiac. He earned a Master's degree in math from Harvard before he turned 20 and went on to teach the subject at MIT and UC-Santa Cruz.

Dickie Goodman made a music career with a microphone and a razor blade. He inter-spliced short snippets of up-and-coming pop hits with his own voice (as a reporter or interviewer), spawning a long series of novelty singles, beginning with "The Flying Saucer" in 1956.

Odd Flowers

The world's smallest flowering plant is the *Wolffia globosa*. Found in tropical climates (including California, Florida, and Hawaii), the blossom is so tiny that a "bouquet" of 12 of them could fit on the head of a pin.

The flowers of mature Venus flytrap plants bloom on a tall stalk far above the carnivorous leaves. They have to; otherwise, the plant would "eat" insects trying to pollinate the flower.

The white and black varieties of the "bat plant," members of the genus *Tacca*, exhibit beautiful flowers with long "whiskers" that may be green or even purple.

The *Raffelesia arnoldii* is famous not only as the plant with the world's largest bloom (three feet across) but also one that reeks of rotting flesh. This odor attracts flies that help pollinate the blossom.

By contrast, the yellow flowers of the box-leaf azara tree have a decidedly better odor: that of vanilla and/or chocolate.

Native to South Africa, the *Ceropegia ampliata* is one of the most visually striking plants when it blooms in "inflated, balloon-like flowers of white and yellow pinstripes, topped with emerald green birdcages."

Onions

The ancient Egyptians were enamored with onions, believing them to be signs of eternity. Not only were onions left in the tombs of pharaohs (presumably to enjoy in the afterlife), but also paintings depicting the vegetables could be found on the inner walls of pyramids.

The Onion is best digested with a grain of salt. Many urban legends and Internet hoaxes have been perpetuated when articles published by this news parody source fooled readers who (for whatever reason) didn't get the joke.

Other ancient cultures also held the onion in high esteem. Both Roman gladiators and Greek athletes rubbed their bodies with onions, believing it helped keep the muscles firm.

Onions are the first add-on item in the famous "hash brown sequence" that is part of the menu at Waffle House restaurants. You can order potatoes in any combination of *scattered* (on the grill), *smothered* (with onions), *covered* (with cheese), *chunked* (with ham), *diced* (with tomatoes), *peppered* (with jalapenos), *capped* (with mushrooms), and *topped* (with chili).

Are the lyrics to The Beatles' song "Glass Onion" filled with mysterious imagery and odd clues? Hardly, according to John Lennon. In interviews, he admitted to adding nonsensical words and phrases in humorous response to the fans who had begun to think that all The Beatles' songs had some "deeper meaning." (In Britain, "glass onion" is a slang term for a monocle.)

In Toombs County, Georgia, farmer Mose Coleman had a hard time giving away the onions he grew in 1931, as they exhibited an unusually sweet taste. After offering them at cut-rate prices, he found that the same customers kept coming back for more of them. The variety is now known as the Vidalia onion.

Opera

The word *opera* is the plural of "opus" (although "opuses" is sometimes used as well). It derives from the Latin for "work."

Several renditions of "Theme from the Three Penny Opera" hit the Pop Top 40 under one of three different titles. Some listed the song as "Moritat" and others by the name probably most familiar to listeners: "Mack the Knife."

Is it possible for an opera singer to break a glass by singing a high note? Theoretically, yes, but the pitch would have to be exact, the volume of the voice would have to be at a high level, and the note would have to be sustained for the proper length of time. (It's easier if the glass is made of crystal.)

Eighteen-year-old Gene Rayburn came to New York with a dream of singing opera. Instead, he got a job as an NBC page, and after a stint in the Air Force during World War II, he parlayed the connections he'd made into a career on radio and TV. He's best known as the host of TV's *Match Game*.

Belle "Bubbles" Silverman performed on New York radio when she was four, and by the time she was seven, she'd adopted a Hollywood-sounding stage name that would serve her well. As Beverly Sills, she went on to play an instrumental role in making opera accessible to the American masses.

The oldest opera house in the United States is Philadelphia's Academy of Music, which celebrated its 150th anniversary in 2007.

Original Names of States

No matter where you are in the United States, the land on which you're standing was once known as something *other* than what it's now called. Here's a short list of some former colonies, republics, and territories that are now parts of states.

Once Known As:	All/Part of What Is Now:
Aquidneck Island (colony)	Rhode Island
Cimarron (territory)	Oklahoma
Deseret (territory)	Utah
Jefferson (territory)	Colorado
Kanawha (republic)	West Virginia
New Connecticut (colony)	Vermont
New Haven (colony)	Connecticut
New Netherlands (colony)	New York
New Sweden (colony)	Delaware
Orleans (territory)	Louisiana
Plymouth (colony)	Massachusetts
Transylvania (colony)	Kentucky

Palindromes

Here is a short list of short words that are called *palindromes*, meaning they read the same backward as forward. And hey, it's just plain funny to say them out loud in order:

- bib, bob, boob
- civic

- dad, deed, did, dud
- eve, ewe, eye
- gag, gig
- kayak, kook
- level
- madam, minim, mom, mum
- noon, nun
- pap, peep, pep, pip, poop, pop, pup
- radar, refer, rotor
- sis
- tat, tenet, tit, toot, tot
- wow

Pants

In most areas of Britain, those who refer to "pants" are actually talking about underwear. Across the pond, what we call pants, Brits refer to as "trousers."

If you're a late-night TV watcher, the name Worldwide Pants might sound familiar to you. It's the name of David Letterman's production company. (Why call it Worldwide Pants? "Worldwide Toupee isn't as catchy."). The organization's hits have included not only the comedian's own talk shows but also the sitcom *Everybody Loves Raymond*.

Before "designer jeans" became a catch phrase, Dittos were the "must-have" slacks of the early 1970s. Unlike Levi's, Dittos were sold in a rainbow of colors and were specially stitched to flatter the female physique.

Sources indicate that the first recorded use of the word "pants" (instead of "pantaloons") in America appeared in the Edgar Allan Poe story "Peter Pendulum, the Business Man," published in an 1840 edition of *Burton's Gentleman's Magazine*.

Technically speaking, the *fly* on a man's trousers isn't the zipper itself, but the flap that folds over it. The name carried over from the nickname for a tent flap, which resembled a wing and flapped in the wind.

In 1966, Best Actress winner Julie Christie became the first high-profile female to wear pants to the Academy Awards. *Time* magazine described her outfit as a "gold lamé pajama suit."

Peanuts

While the *Peanuts* have collectively appeared in various commercials for Dolly Madison snack cakes, Metropolitan Life insurance, and the like, the character known as Pig Pen got his own gig in 1993, starring in spots for Regina vacuum cleaners.

Peanuts creator Charles M. Schulz seemed destined for a career in the comics. As an infant, an uncle gave him a nickname that stuck with him for the rest of his life: Sparky, short for Sparkplug, which was the name of Barney Google's horse.

On May 5, 2007, a comic book containing more than 100 *Peanuts* strips not seen since their initial run was given away free by retailers around the world as part of the Free Comic Book Day celebration.

Charles Schulz was said to be upset in 1950 when he learned that, in order to "go national," United Press Syndicate changed the title of his comic strip from *Li'l Folks* to *Peanuts* to avoid confusion with another similarly named series.

In *Peanuts*, when Charlie Brown's younger sister, Sally, was found to be suffering from amblyopia ("lazy eye"), the U.S. Department of Health, Education, and Welfare commissioned creator Charles Schulz to come up with an informational pamphlet titled "Security Is an Eye Patch."

Bookstores are filled with comic-strip compilations, but it wasn't always that way. The first one, which was published by Rinehart & Company, was a 1952 grouping of some of the earliest *Peanuts* strips.

Perfume and Cologne

The first Avon Lady was no lady at all. It was David McConnell, a book salesman who gave small bottles of perfume to housewives who would allow him inside their homes to listen to his pitch. He soon realized that there was a market for door-to-door cosmetic sales, particularly in rural areas.

On February 26, 1996, Elizabeth Taylor appeared on four different CBS sitcoms as a promotion for her then-new perfume, Black Pearls: *Can't Hurry Love*, *High Society*, *Murphy Brown*, and *The Nanny*.

Just like the Oscars and the Emmys, the Fragrance Foundation holds an annual awards ceremony—the FiFis.

In the seventeenth century, most gentlemen kept perfume in the heads of their walking sticks. A quick whiff would ward off the nasty street smells of that era.

Charisma Carpenter, who found fame first as a cheerleader for the San Diego Chargers and then on TV's *Buffy the Vampire Slayer*, was named after an Avon perfume (much to her alleged dismay).

In 1979, Shelley Hack was tapped to replace Kate Jackson on *Charlie's Angels* based solely on her high profile as the spokesmodel for Revlon's Charlie perfume.

The first fragrance marketed exclusively for males was Estee Lauder's Aramis, which was launched in 1964.

Pest Control

The first useful application for aerosol spray cans was introduced during World War II. Insecticide-filled "bug bombs," as they were called, helped protect American military personnel from disease-carrying insects.

In the first season of the sitcom *Full House*, John Stamos's character was an exterminator named Jesse Cochran. He later found a better job as a jingle writer and rock musician and a decidedly more Greek last name: Katsopolis.

Guitarist Greg Ginn of punk band Black Flag revealed that, although the band's moniker wasn't specifically inspired by the popular brand of insect-control products, they didn't mind the connection: "It just sounded, you know, heavy."

Through the mid-twentieth century, untold ecological damage occurred after several nations began purposely spreading oil over mosquito-infested swamps in order to reduce the spread of malaria.

Marvin Glass and Associates designed the original *Mouse Trap* board game that Ideal sold in 1963. However, the company refused to pay any royalties or licensing fees to Rube Goldberg, even though the game's elaborate mousetrap resembled one of his cartoons.

Green Acres star Eddie Albert was also an ardent environmentalist and one of the first people to call for a ban on DDT. In 1969, he sailed to Anacapa Island to study the pelicans there and found that chicks were dying because the pesticide had caused mothers to lay eggs with shells that were too fragile.

Some establishments nail water-filled plastic bags over their outer doorways in order to repel flies. The theory is that the compound eye of the fly spies the moving reflections in the bag and shies away, thinking it's a predator of some sort.

Pianos

Yamaha eventually became known as one of the more popular Japanese motorcycle brands, but the company has been doing what it does best—producing pianos—for more than 120 years.

We've all seen comedy routines in which the hinged cover protecting a piano's keyboard falls on the fingers of the person playing it. The proper name of this contraption is a *fallboard*.

While many of those who play piano in motion pictures are faking, that's not always the case. Notable exceptions of pianists who performed "for real" include Holly Hunter in *The Piano*, Richard Gere in *Pretty Woman*, and Dudley Moore in *Arthur*.

Except for a few variations in color, the basic design of the piano keyboard has remained the same since 1450.

The piano on which John Lennon composed the classic "Imagine" was sold at auction in 2000 and was purchased by singer George Michael. It was sent on a symbolic "peace tour" of the United States in 2007.

The toy piano was invented in Philadelphia in 1872 by German immigrant Albert Schoenhut. It was meant to provide educational entertainment for children but has since been used as an instrument in many serious compositions.

Pigs

Actress Eva Gabor wasn't necessarily upset that she wasn't the *Green Acres* character to receive the most fan mail week-in and week-out, but she was never comfortable in the knowledge that she was second only to Arnold the Pig.

If the thought of eating pigs' feet doesn't strike your fancy, you might choose to refer to the dish by its more eloquent name: *pettitoes*.

Saint Paul, the capital of Minnesota, had a decidedly less dignified name when it was first settled in the early nineteenth century. The town was then known as Pig's Eye Landing, named after a local trader Pierre "Pig's Eye" Parrant.

Before scientists found a way to develop a synthetic version of the hormone, diabetics were treated with insulin derived from pig pancreata.

While pigs were once used to help sniff out valuable truffles from the ground, dogs are just as well equipped for the job and are more commonly used today.

Even though people complain on hot days that they're "sweating like a pig," porkers don't perspire. In fact, hog farms in warmer areas have to install sprinklers to keep the pigs cool.

Pinball

Pinball machines and video games were banned in New York City from 1942 until 1976. The city's lawmakers felt they were nothing more than gambling devices that owed more to luck than to skill.

The only positive aspect of the 1979 film flop *Tilt* (starring a young Brooke Shields) that critics could find was the then-groundbreaking "point of view" photography from the inside of a pinball machine.

The sequence makes sense. First there were the arcade video games *Pac-Man* and *Ms. Pac-Man*, then a pinball machine called *Mr. & Mrs. Pac-Man*. The next natural step was the 1982 hybrid known as *Baby Pac-Man*, which was half video game and half pinball machine.

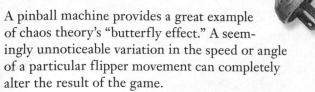

A pinball machine provides a great example of chaos theory's "butterfly effect." A seemingly unnoticeable variation in the speed or angle of a particular flipper movement can completely alter the result of the game.

The *tilt* feature that keeps players from overmanipulating a pinball game by using too much "body English" was originally called *stool pigeon*.

While Elton John played a specially constructed machine for his role as the Pinball Wizard in the 1975 film *Tommy*, Roger Daltrey unleashed his supple wrist on a classic Gottlieb game called *Kings and Queens*.

Pizza

In the United States, pepperoni is the overwhelming favorite addition to a cheese pizza. In Japan, seafood (eel and squid) is a popular choice, while green peas are added to the mix in Brazil. In Costa Rica, pizza pies are often topped with coconut.

The Pizza Hut restaurant chain got its name when the first location opened in Wichita in 1957. The sign only had space for three more letters besides "Pizza," and because the restaurant building resembled a hut, the choice was a natural one.

Modern pizza (also known as *pizza margherita*) is made with tomatoes, mozzarella cheese, and basil—thought to represent the three colors (red, white, and green) of the flag of Italy.

Benjamin Salisbury, who found success as son Brighton Sheffield on the sitcom *The Nanny*, played a Domino's delivery person on a series of TV commercials in 2006, promoting the chain's short-lived Fudgem brownies.

It's not delivery; it's DiGiorno (introduced nationally in 1996) that stormed onto the scene to become the top-selling frozen pizza in the United States. Its "rising crust" has helped the brand rise to claim nearly 20 percent of the market. Perennial favorites Red Baron and Tombstone are the next biggest brand names.

Carmela Bitale became an unknown hero to millions in 1983 when she patented her "package saver for pizza and cakes." It's the tiny plastic stand used by pizza take-out and delivery services that helps keep the top of the cardboard box from sticking to the pizza.

Plumbing

Jane Withers, who promoted Comet cleanser on television as Josephine the Plumber, was a child star. Her first film appearance was opposite Shirley Temple in 1934's *Bright Eyes*.

Using a Maytag washing machine motor, some roller skate wheels, and a combination of special blades, Samuel Blanc devised a machine in 1935 that would cut tree roots out of sewer lines without doing any digging. His wife christened the gadget Roto-Rooter.

On FOX TV's *Married ... with Children*, man's man Al Bundy designed what he called the ultimate man's bathroom, which featured five toilet paper dispensers, no sink, and the "Mighty Ferguson."

Even if you've never driven a Buick, you've probably sat in one. David Dunbar Buick developed a process to bond porcelain onto cast iron and gave the world the modern bathtub.

While the toilet in the kids' bathroom on *The Brady Bunch* was never seen, the one on *Leave It to Beaver* played a key role in an early episode, when Wally and Beaver hid a baby alligator in the device's tank.

What esteemed genius once reportedly said that if he had it all to do over again, he'd become a plumber? None other than Albert Einstein.

Poetry

Stanley Kunitz, Billy Collins, Louise Gluck, Ted Kooser, and Donald Hall—if you don't know these names, you're not alone. But give them their due: they're the men and women who have held the position of U.S. Poet Laureate since the year 2000.

While the title of the Lydia Child poem "The Boy's Thanksgiving Day" might not ring a bell, it's very likely the work's opening line will: "Over the river and through the woods / to grandmother's house we go …"

The Book of Counted Sorrows is a poetry collection that Dean Koontz regularly refers to in his novels. This elusive book didn't exist until 2003 when, after thousands of requests from readers, he published it in a limited edition.

Nipsey Russell was referred to as "The Poet Laureate of Television." The game show regular was known for his witty four-line verses. He said writing them was easy; he began with the punch line and went backward from there.

Haiku is old, but not as ancient as you might think. While much of Japan's culture and tradition can be traced back as much as 2,500 years, five/seven/five-syllable haiku poetry "only" dates back to the fifteenth century.

Oddly, *syphilis* got its name from a poem. In 1530, physician Girolamo Fracastoro wrote a poem titled "Syphilis" about a young shepherd who was the first person afflicted with the disease, and the title became the common name for the STD.

Post Office

In 1978, the USPS began offering first-class stamps marked with a letter code "A" instead of its denomination, 15 cents. The code advanced with rate increases as follows: "B" (18 cents, in 1981), "C" (20 cents, later in 1981), "D" (22 cents, 1985), "E" (25 cents, 1988), "F" (29 cents, 1991), "G" (32 cents, 1994) and finally "H" (33 cents, 1999). The series was then discontinued.

Few Americans take advantage of the Media Mail rate available at the local post office. Media items (books, audio and video recordings, CDs and DVDs, and more) that are not considered advertising materials may be sent at a much cheaper rate than first-class mail.

By sending an envelope and money for postage to the postmaster at a post office where a stamp is being issued, you can receive free First Day Covers, which are specially postmarked "first day of issue" and are considered collectible.

In 1975, a unique tie-in allowed post offices in both the United States and the Soviet Union to sell two pairs of stamps with the same design. They were issued in honor of the Apollo-Soyuz space mission that year, in which crafts from the two nations linked together and shared time in space.

Canada uses two-letter postal abbreviations just like the United States. Here's the list: Alberta (AB), British Columbia (BC), Manitoba (MB),

New Brunswick (NB), Newfoundland and Labrador (NF), Northwest Territories (NT), Nova Scotia (NS), Nunavut (NU), Ontario (ON), Prince Edward Island (PE), Quebec (PC or QC), Saskatchewan (SK), and Yukon Territory (YT).

Flat-rate Priority Mail is a bargain for items that fit the post office's requirements. If a 70-pound item fits into one of the two flat-rate box sizes provided by the USPS, you can send it cross-country for under $10. Using Priority Mail to send a larger item of the same weight will cost many times as much over the same distance.

Potatoes

In 1944, the H.W. Lay Company became one of the first snack food makers to advertise on television, with a cartoon character called Oscar, the Happy Potato. It was never explained how Oscar was happy to be sliced wafer-thin and deep-fried in a vat of boiling oil.

Sweet potatoes aren't potatoes at all, but vine roots. They're also unrelated to yams.

After 35 years of puffing, Mr. Potato Head officially gave up his pipe in 1987 in conjunction with the American Cancer Society's Great American Smokeout.

Ore-Ida, the leading potato processor in the United States, is named for the Oregon/Idaho border, where most potatoes are grown. The company made a miscue in 2002 when they attempted to lure kids with colored *Funky Kool* French fries to match the colorful ketchup being produced by Heinz.

How did diminutive NBA star Anthony "Spud" Webb garner his tuber-iffic name? Turns out, it had nothing to do with potatoes. It was short for Sputnik, a nickname his grandmother had given him as a child.

To further distance themselves from other brands, Pringles began officially referring to its product as "potato crisps" in 1991.

Presidential Afflictions

In September 1955, Dwight Eisenhower became the first sitting president to suffer a heart attack. He'd complained of indigestion while playing golf on the afternoon of September 23 and went to bed that evening still complaining of pain. He was rushed to the hospital sometime after 2 A.M. on September 24.

Ronald Reagan began wearing a hearing aid in 1983; he'd lost a significant amount of hearing on a film set back in 1940 when a fellow actor fired a pistol near his head.

Jimmy Carter's particularly personal ailment would've remained his own little secret had it not been for the good intentions of his friend Anwar

Sadat. The Egyptian president announced to the world on December 24, 1978, that his good friend Jimmy had hemorrhoids and made a public appeal for all Egyptians to pray for his swift recovery.

Cigar-smoker Grover Cleveland was diagnosed with oral cancer in 1893. At his insistence, his ailment was kept secret, and surgery to correct the condition was performed aboard his yacht. This way, he didn't have to check into a hospital, and the press was never alerted to his condition.

Richard Nixon was first diagnosed with phlebitis in 1965. The condition later led to blood clots in his leg and on his lung.

In 1919, Woodrow Wilson suffered a catastrophic stroke that was hidden from the press and public. In truth, this was Wilson's third stroke; he'd suffered from atherosclerosis and bad teeth, a potentially deadly combination.

Pro Sports on the Move

It used to be that pro sports teams would occasionally move from one city to another. Today, the trend seems to be for a city to lose a team and then either steal one from another town or be awarded a brand new franchise a few years later. Here are some examples from recent memory:

- Atlanta Flames (NHL, moved to Calgary 1980)
  Atlanta Thrashers (NHL, new franchise 1999)

- Baltimore Colts (NFL, moved to Indiana-polis 1984)
  Baltimore Ravens (NFL, moved from Cleveland 1996)
- Cleveland Browns (NFL, moved to Balti-more 1996)
  Cleveland Browns (NFL, new franchise 1999)
- Charlotte Hornets (NBA, moved to New Orleans 2002)
  Charlotte Bobcats (NBA, new franchise 2004)
- Colorado Rockies (NHL, moved to New Jersey 1982)
  Colorado Avalanche (NHL, moved from Quebec 1995)
- Houston Oilers (NFL, moved to Tennessee 1997)
  Houston Texans (NFL, new franchise 2002)
- Minnesota North Stars (NHL, moved to Dallas 1993)
  Minnesota Wild (NHL, new franchise 2000)
- New Orleans Jazz (NBA, moved to Utah 1979)
  New Orleans Hornets (NBA, moved from Charlotte 2002)
- St. Louis Cardinals (NFL, moved to Phoenix 1988)
  St. Louis Rams (NFL, moved from Los Angeles 1995)

- Washington Senators (MLB, moved to
  Minnesota 1960)
  Washington Senators (MLB, new franchise
  1961)
- Washington Senators (MLB, moved to Texas
  1972)
  Washington Nationals (MLB, moved from
  Montreal 2005)

Of course, there's also the Oakland Raiders, who
moved from Oakland to Los Angeles in 1982, but
then returned to Oakland in 1995.

Proprietary Eponyms A to Z

Here's an A-to-Z list of brands/products that are
(or once were) trademarked names:

- Aspirin
- Breathalyzer, Brassiere, Baggies, Beer Nuts,
  Bubble Wrap
- Claymation, Cellophane, Crayola
- Dumpster, Dry Ice
- Escalator
- Frisbee, Freon
- Granola, Gunk
- Heroin, Hula-Hoop
- iPod
- Jacuzzi, Jockey Shorts, Jaws of Life, Jeep
- Kerosene, Kitty Litter

- Laundromat, Linoleum, LP Record
- Mace, Magic Marker, Muzak
- Novocain
- Ouija
- Popsicle, Pop-Tart
- Q-Tip
- Rollerblade, Rolodex, Realtor
- Styrofoam, Sheetrock, Scotch Tape, Swiss Army Knife
- Tabloid, Thermos, Teflon, Trampoline
- Velcro
- Windbreaker, Walkman
- Xerox
- Yo-Yo
- Zipper

PSA Icons

Due to the similarity between his last name and that of canine PSA character McGruff, who urges everyone to "take a bite out of crime," baseball slugger Fred McGriff became popularly known among fans as "The Crime Dog."

Woodsy Owl debuted in 1970 as an environmental representative who chastised us "Give a hoot, don't pollute," a slogan coined by U.S. Forest Ranger Chuck Williams. During the 1990s, Woodsy's message was changed to be a bit more all encompassing: "Lend a hand, care for the land!"

Dick Van Dyke starred in a series of Public Service Announcements from 1975 to 1984 for the National Fire Protection Agency's "Learn Not to Burn" campaign. After he lost his Malibu home to a wildfire, he agreed to become the voice of Sparky, the Fire Dog.

Before there was a rock band of the same name, there were the original Crash Test Dummies. Named Larry and Vince, these two characters spent 15 years reminding Americans what could happen to them if they forget to buckle their seat belts when riding in an automobile. Their motto: "You could learn a lot from a dummy."

There's an old children's joke about Smokey the Bear's middle name being "The." Not only is the joke bad, but the information is as well. The character's full name is really just Smokey Bear.

Purple

While most believe that "The Purple People Eater" is a purple creature that eats people, the novelty song hit's lyrics reveal a different story. In them, the rock 'n' roll monster reveals that he enjoys "eatin' purple people." Fans are divided on the issue.

George Washington first offered the Badge for Military Merit, better known as the Purple Heart. It was originally a heart-shaped cloth patch attached to the uniform. In 1932, to commemorate the bicentennial of Washington's birth, the award was reintroduced as a medal presented to U.S. military personnel injured during combat.

The author of *Harold and the Purple Crayon* felt that his name might be too difficult for youngsters to pronounce properly, so David Leisk published the popular children's book under the pen name Crockett Johnson.

Those who disliked the Barney the Dinosaur character came up with all sorts of hateful nicknames for the character, perhaps the most bizarre of which was "The Purple Antichrist."

Where are the "purple mountain majesties" referred to in the patriotic song "America, the Beautiful"? Katharine Lee Bates wrote the lyrics in 1893 when she viewed her surroundings from the summit of Pike's Peak.

Porphyrophobia is defined as the irrational and persistent fear of the color purple.

Radio Personalities

In 2001, after hearing deterioration in his voice, listeners learned that conservative radio voice Rush Limbaugh was suffering from near-complete hearing loss. Cochlear implant surgery at year's end helped to improve both his hearing ability and thus his ability to enunciate properly.

Best known as red-haired, freckle-faced Danny on TV's *The Partridge Family*, Danny Bonaduce has found a second career as a radio personality. So far, the job has sent him on a virtual zigzag tour of the country, with stops at Philadelphia, Phoenix, Chicago, Detroit, New York, and Los Angeles, in that order.

Long-time Los Angeles disc jockey Jim Ladd provided the voice of the DJ for the 1987 album *Radio KAOS* by former Pink Floyd frontman Roger Waters. He also appeared in videos for the album's singles and traveled with Waters on tour, performing the role in concerts from a radio booth high above the stage.

When DJ Robert Smith first adopted the professional name Wolfman Jack, he shied away from public appearances because he couldn't decide how the Wolfman should look.

The Rest of the Story's radio legend Paul Harvey is credited with coining the words "guesstimate" and "Reaganomics."

Iva Ikuko Toguri was born in Los Angeles but found herself stranded in Tokyo while visiting relatives in 1941 after Pearl Harbor was bombed. She was drafted into work as a disc jockey for Radio

Tokyo, and while the rest of the world called her Tokyo Rose, she only ever referred to herself as Orphan Ann.

Reader's Digest

Reader's Digest began life in 1922 as a 25-cent publication available only by mail, printed in the Greenwich Village apartment of DeWitt and Lila Wallace. Alexander Graham Bell wrote the lead article in the first issue, and the magazine became available on newsstands seven years later.

With just over 10 million in paid circulation, *Reader's Digest* is the top-selling magazine in the United States *not* published by the American Association of Retired Persons. Worldwide circulation is double that, with an estimated 100 million readers globally.

Reader's Digest is one of the few magazines whose popularity calls for publication in the United States in multiple editions. Along with the standard magazine, *Reader's Digest* is also offered in a Spanish language version and a Large Type version for visually impaired readers.

If you hope to collect every copy of *Reader's Digest* ever published, you'd better start building those shelves. The December 2007 edition of the magazine will be its 1,028th issue.

Now known as *Select Editions, Reader's Digest* has offered readers *Condensed Book* selections since 1950. A major controversy arose in 1982, when *Reader's Digest* published a condensed version of The Bible that shortened the Old Testament by 50 percent and the New Testament by 25 percent.

Until 1955, no advertisements appeared in U.S. editions of *Reader's Digest*. What's more, the magazine has always prohibited advertising for tobacco products, a rule the publication still enforces today.

Rings

While it's true that Richard Starkey earned the stage name Ringo Starr due to the rings he wore on his fingers, that isn't the whole story. He first began using the moniker in 1958 as drummer for a group known as the Raving Texans, and part of the appeal was the Old West flavor of the "Ringo" name.

Saturn's rings are by far the most visible, but rings also surround the other outer planets—Jupiter, Uranus, and Neptune.

When the Great Depression hit, jewelry makers did what they could to stay afloat in an era when displays of wealth were frowned upon. For engagement rings, this involved designing multifaceted settings for diamonds that made the stones appear much larger than they actually were, keeping them affordable.

The combined cost of the three *Lord of the Rings* films exceeded $300 million, and investors were wary of the risk involved. The worldwide box office take for the three films, of course, proved most pleasing to everyone involved in the project. The total was just short of *$3 billion*, making it the top movie trilogy of all time.

Of the more than 500 "active" volcanoes on Earth, three quarters of them lie in an area called the "Ring of Fire" that forms a chain around the Pacific Ocean. The area includes western North and South America, from Alaska all the way to Chile.

In 1913, IOC founder Pierre de Coubertin designed the Olympic logo still in use today, depicting five interlocking rings of blue, yellow, black, green, and red. The rings represent (in no particular order) the continents participating in the games: Africa, America, Asia, Australia, and Europe.

Rivers

Some of the longest rivers in the world have the shortest names, including the Amur, the Don, the Kama, the Lena, the Nile, the Ob, the Syr, the Ural, and the Xi, all of which flow for more than 1,000 miles.

The Mississippi is the most important river in the United States and has been for centuries. In fact, the name comes from the Algonquin phrase "missi sipi," which means, quite simply, "large river."

Just four years after the 1972 film *Deliverance* hit theaters, 24 canoeists were killed attempting to traverse the same treacherous parts of the Chattooga River depicted in the movie.

Who painted the image that appears on the cover of Billy Joel's 1993 album *River of Dreams?* None other than the Piano Man's then-wife, Christie Brinkley.

The answer to the question "What is the largest river on Earth?" depends on your definition of "largest." While the Nile is the longest at nearly 6,700 miles, the slightly shorter Amazon contains much more actual water and drains a much larger area.

Her face isn't the only thing that's changed: Joan Rivers' real last name is Molinsky. And, for good measure, while River Phoenix's first name was indeed River, his last name was originally Bottom.

Road Signs

The maximum speed limit you'll see on U.S. highway signs depends on the state. In Iowa, New

Mexico, and North and South Dakota, 75 mph is posted on some stretches of interstate highways. But in Hawaii, 60 mph is the maximum statewide, and in the District of Columbia, 55 mph is still the law.

The criteria vary from state to state, but as a rule, each area works closely with the Department of Natural Resources to review reported automobile/deer accidents. A "Deer Crossing" sign is generally erected wherever a deer has been hit within the previous 12 months.

Forty-nine states participate in the "Adopt a Highway" program. The lone holdout is Vermont, whose antibillboard laws prohibit the necessary road adoption signage.

In 2004, the Federal Highway Administration approved the use of a new font, Clearview, on federal road signs after tests showed that drivers found Clearview easier to read than the current Highway Gothic font.

Those large blue signs on freeways indicating that there's a Shell station or a McDonald's at the next exit are called "interstate logo boards." A business must meet strict criteria, such as restrooms, telephones, no cover charge, and so on, in order to get its name posted.

The Federal Highway Administration has adopted certain shapes for the various types of road signs in hopes that drivers will recognize them reflexively.

A round sign indicates a railroad crossing; a pentagon stands for a school crossing; and diamond-shaped signs alert us to a particular potential hazard.

Rocks

The back of the New Hampshire state quarter depicts The Old Man of the Mountain, a natural rock formation that resembled the face of an elderly male and served as the state's emblem. We say "resembled" and "served" because, sadly, the formation collapsed off the side of Cannon Mountain on May 3, 2003.

The Prudential Insurance Company began using the slogan "We have the strength of Gibraltar" back in 1896 and has employed an image of the Rock of Gibraltar as its logo ever since.

The oldest rocks found on the earth's surface are located near the Great Slave Lake in the Northwestern Territories of Canada. Dating methods have estimated the age of some of the zircon crystals at between 4 and 4.4 billion years.

Like many legends of early America, Plymouth Rock is very likely just that—a legend. The first written record of the stone as the spot where passengers stepped off the Mayflower was published more than a century afterward.

Ireland's famous Blarney Stone, said to bring "eloquence" to anyone who kisses it, has attracted millions of visitors from around the world. Unconfirmed reports reveal that locals have long entered Blarney Castle after hours to "deface" the stone by urinating on it.

Revealing that Americans will buy nearly anything, for the 1975 holiday season, Gary Dahl packaged small, tumbled stones in boxes with an accompanying training manual and offered them as "pet rocks" for $3.95 each. By the time Christmas arrived, he had sold over 1 million of them.

Roles Turned Down

Comic Jerry Van Dyke (Dick's brother) had two sitcom offers on the table in 1965 but sadly chose the wrong character. He felt that being the son of a porter in *My Mother, the Car* was preferable to playing the bumbling first mate on *Gilligan's Island*.

Diminutive actor Mickey Rooney was first offered the role of Archie Bunker on TV's *All in the Family*. However, The Mick soundly refused the role, saying that the obnoxious bigot was "un-American" and that the job would prove to be career suicide for anyone who took it.

Steven Spielberg and George Lucas wanted Tom Selleck for the role of Indiana Jones, but Selleck had already committed to the TV series *Magnum, P.I.*, and the producers wouldn't give him the necessary time off.

The role of tough-girl Rizzo in the 1978 film *Grease* was originally offered to Lucie Arnaz, with the proviso that she took a screen test first. However, mama Lucille Ball declared that testing was beneath her famous offspring, so the part went to Stockard Channing.

Chevy Chase rejected the lead role of Lester Burnham in the *American Beauty* script because he didn't "get it," plus he feared such a role would tarnish his "family friendly" image. Of course, Kevin Spacey won an Oscar for his portrayal of the character.

Henry Fonda played the patriarch in the film *Spencer's Mountain*, which served as the pilot for the TV series *The Waltons*. He was offered the role of Pa Walton, but after reading several scripts, he surmised that the star of the show was John-Boy, not the dad, and turned it down.

The Rolling Stones

In 1968, when the Democratic National Convention was held in Chicago, Mayor Richard Daley asked radio stations across the city to refrain from playing the Rolling Stones' song "Street Fighting Man" so as not to incite rioters.

Which came first, the Rolling Stones or *Rolling Stone* magazine? The band predated the bi-weekly periodical by five years.

The Stones keep getting richer for doing less work, at least on stage. In 1989, they set a world record by grossing $98 million during a 60-concert tour. In 2005, their tour lasted only 42 shows, but the band brought in an amazing $162 million, setting a new record.

Thanks in part to socialized dentistry and also substance abuse, Keith Richard's smile was in such disrepair during the 1970s that one of his teeth reportedly fell out during a magazine interview.

An unlikely defender of the Rolling Stones was Bob Dylan. In some poetry printed in the liner notes of his album *Another Side of Bob Dylan*, the folk-rock star suggested that Dean Martin should apologize to the Stones. Martin had made the band the butt of many jokes on his TV variety show.

In 1977, Margaret Trudeau, wife of Canadian Prime Minister Pierre Trudeau, left her own anniversary party to see the Rolling Stones play in Toronto. She returned with them to their hotel for a night of partying and later accompanied guitarist Ron Wood back to England for a time.

Roman Numerals

The year 1988 had the longest Roman numeral sequence of any year since such numbers were used: MCMLXXXVIII. Twelve years later came the shortest one in recent history: MM for the year 2000.

A Roman numeral added to a name to indicate its order in succession, as in England's kings George I, George II, and George III, is known as an *ordinal*.

A line above a Roman numeral indicates that the amount represented should be multiplied by 1,000.

The famous Mark VII Limited productions logo was made by a man's hands hammering a metal stamp with the number "VII." The hands holding the hammer and stamp are those of the production company's founder, *Dragnet* star Jack Webb.

Some retailers ran into problems stocking clothing to promote the 2006 Super Bowl. The Roman numerals attached to the proper name of the event—*Super Bowl XL*—created confusion for those who mistook the letters as an abbreviation for "extra large." (The same may occur again in 2016 for Super Bowl L.)

Many clocks depicting Roman numerals show the number four as "IIII" instead of "IV." Historians are divided on how this tradition developed, blaming it on everything from the desires of King Louis XIV (who was convinced that "IV" was incorrect) to better symmetry on the clock's face.

Roseanne

On the sitcom, the Conners live at 714 Delaware Street, near the corner of Third. Babe Ruth wore jersey #3, hit 714 home runs in his pro career, and John Goodman (Dan Conner on *Roseanne*) played *The Babe* in a 1992 feature film. Do you think there's a coincidence here?

Roseanne Conner's fourth child was supposed to be a girl and was even announced as such after an amniocentesis, but when Grateful Dead singer Jerry Garcia died suddenly, Roseanne Barr decided to honor him by making her TV baby a boy and naming it after him.

Johnny Galecki's character was introduced as Kevin when he first appeared on the show. When he was added as a regular cast member, however, his name was changed to David because he'd been under contract playing a character named Kevin on another show.

The late Glenn Quinn was born and raised in Ireland. He had to adopt an American accent in order to earn the role of Mark Healy, husband of eldest daughter Becky Conner.

Laurie Metcalf (as Roseanne's sister, Jackie Harris) eventually married Matt Roth, the actor who played her abusive boyfriend Fisher. Metcalf's real-life daughter from her first marriage, Zoe Perry, also appeared on one episode of *Roseanne*—she played a young Jackie.

John Goodman wanted to leave the show after the eighth season, which was supposed to be the final season for *Roseanne*. When the series was picked up for one more season, the producers decided to have Dan Conner suffer a heart attack, so that there'd be an excuse for his character's limited appearances in season nine.

Skateboarding

Although the fad didn't take off until the 1970s, the first skateboards were mass-produced back in the 1950s, when the sport was promoted as "sidewalk surfing."

The development of polyurethane wheels and the addition of kickplates to the back of skateboards are the two key factors that led to increased interest in skateboarding in the mid-1970s. The improvements allowed riders to travel faster and with more control than ever before.

Before he found success on *Saturday Night Live*, David Spade worked at a skateboard shop. In fact, his talent on the device helped him land his first film role, that of a young skateboarding punk named Kyle in *Police Academy 4: Citizens on Patrol*.

Among celebrities who have broken bones while riding ... er, *attempting* to ride a skateboard are dancer Fred Astaire, comedian Tom Green, and guitarist Brian May.

Of course, celebrities aren't the only ones who take the occasional spill. Despite improved safety measures, including helmets and pads for knees and elbows, as many as 80,000 emergency room visits annually in the United States are the result of skateboarding mishaps.

It is estimated that more than one third of the approximately 9 million skateboarders in the United States live in California.

Skyscrapers

Newer U.S. cities that have had room to "spread out" tend to have fewer (and smaller) skyscrapers. The tallest building in Phoenix, the sixth-most-populous American city with 1.5 million inhabitants, is only 40 stories tall.

Chinese architects have been reaching for the sky over the last two decades. In 1988, none of the nation's buildings ranked in the top 20 worldwide. Today, China claims 10 of the 20 tallest skyscrapers on the planet. (In addition, a TV tower under construction in Guangzhou is expected to become the first man-made structure to break the 2,000-foot mark.)

While it has been eclipsed as the tallest building in the world, the Sears Tower in Chicago still has more floors—110—than any other skyscraper on Earth.

Besides the Sears Tower, Chicago is home to three other buildings more than 1,000 feet tall: the Aon Center, the John Hancock Center, and the AT&T

Corporate Center. A fourth, Two Prudential Plaza, misses the cut by only 5 feet.

You'll find no skyscrapers of note in our nation's capital. Laws dictate that no structure in the District of Columbia can stand taller than the 555-foot-tall Washington Monument.

When viewing a list of the 20 tallest buildings on Earth, the Empire State Building stands out because of its age. The structure was completed in 1931, nearly 40 years before the next-oldest skyscraper on the list.

The height of the Empire State Building stretches from 1,250 feet to 1,455 feet when you include its antenna. At the very top is a mast that was intended to anchor dirigibles but was never used for that purpose.

Snow

The National Weather Service only classifies a snowstorm as a *blizzard* if it meets certain requirements. The blowing snow must reduce visibility to one-quarter mile or less for at least three hours.

At any given time, snow covers approximately one quarter of the surface of the earth.

Not only does it have to be cold to snow, but snow actually also helps the weather stay chilly. When the white stuff covers the ground, warming rays from the sun are reflected out into space, and heat has difficulty penetrating the ground, keeping temperatures lower.

In centuries past, tales of snow during warm weather have most commonly been attributed to nearby volcanic eruptions, after which white pieces of ash may float from the sky looking like snow.

Snowflakes take various shapes, but all are based on a hexagonal (six-sided) pattern inherent to the crystals in ice. The "arms" of a snowflake are technically known as *dendrites*.

Despite the regular heat, it *does* snow near the equator, but only in the very highest elevations, like 19,340-foot-tall Mount Kilimanjaro in Tanzania.

Soap Operas

The Emmy Awards finally gave daytime shows their own category in 1974. The first show to win for Outstanding Daytime Drama was *The Doctors*, which beat out rivals *Days of Our Lives* and *General Hospital*.

If you think soap operas got their name from the soap companies that advertised heavily during the programs, then you're correct. Advertisers knew that housewives and stay-at-home moms (who tend to be the ones to use most soap products) were a perfect, captive audience for their goods.

The Young and the Restless star Jeanne Cooper underwent a facelift in 1984. She pitched producers the idea of including real filmed footage of the surgery in the show, as if her character (Katherine Chancellor) had experienced the same procedure, and they incorporated it into the soap's storyline.

In the first deal of its kind, the soap opera *Passions* announced in April 2007 that it wasn't being cancelled after all, but that the show would leave NBC, and continue airing new episodes as an exclusive to subscribers of the DirecTV satellite service.

The familiar theme song for the long-running daytime soap *Days of Our Lives* was cowritten by Tommy Boyce and Bobby Hart, who were best known for penning many late-1960s pop hits, including The Monkees' "Last Train to Clarksville."

Bo Derek may have been a *10* in the movies, but her 1998 evening soap opera *Wind on Water* lasted only two episodes before NBC pulled the plug.

Guiding Light broadcast its 15,000th episode in 2006 and celebrated its 55th year on television in 2007, making it the longest-running soap opera in TV history. The drama began as a radio series back in 1937.

Socks

In 1996, Socks Clinton, the First Cat, was featured on a series of nine postage stamps issued by the Central African Republic. While he lived at the White House, Socks befriended a stray tabby who was immediately dubbed Slippers.

Donny Osmond's purple socks started out as a running joke on *The Donny and Marie Show*, but later in his life when he developed obsessive-compulsive disorder, he found he couldn't leave the house without his special hosiery.

At only 5 feet tall, ventriloquist Shari Lewis found a traditional dummy too unwieldy to perform with onstage. She fashioned a sheep puppet out of a sock, and the famous Lamb Chop was born.

If you're not diabetic, you may be uncertain of the purpose of labeling socks as "diabetic socks." The key difference is that they are less binding than regular socks, which is important to those suffering diabetes, because the disease can cause poor circulation in the feet.

Artifacts recovered in northern England in 2005 revealed that ancient Romans who conquered the area committed what is today considered one of the gawkiest of fashion faux pas: they wore wool socks with their sandals.

Carroll O'Connor happened to see Rob Reiner backstage one day getting dressed for rehearsal and noticed that Reiner put a sock and a shoe on one foot, then the same on the other foot. O'Connor yelled at him, "Don't you know that the whole world puts on a sock and a sock and a shoe and a shoe?" This exchange inspired a memorable scene on *All in the Family*.

South Park

South Park hit TV airwaves in 1997, but some of the main characters first appeared five years earlier, when co-creators Trey Parker and Matt Stone used construction paper cutouts to animate a movie short called *The Spirit of Christmas*.

The characters Stan Marsh and Kyle Broflofski represent the show's creators. In fact, the kids' parents in the show share the same first names as Trey and Matt's real-life parents.

Throughout the series and in the *Bigger, Longer & Uncut* movie, all of *South Park*'s Canadian characters have been depicted with "open" heads that move up and down at the mouth as they talk. These include the kids' favorite TV characters, Terrance and Phillip, and Kyle's adopted brother, Ike.

Somewhat surprisingly, *South Park* has garnered fans elsewhere in the world. An online poll held by independent British TV network Channel 4 placed it as the third-best animated series in history, behind *The Simpsons* and *Tom & Jerry*.

In 2006, a falling out between Parker and Stone and Isaac Hayes resulted in the removal of Chef

from the *South Park* cast. The popular character—
who cooked in the bedroom as well as in the
cafeteria—was named Jerome McElroy.

If you'd like to visit the inspiration for the town
of South Park, look no further than Fairplay,
Colorado, in Park County. While you can visit a
museum known as South Park City, don't expect to
see Eric Cartman there—it honors not the show,
but the gold rush that swept the area in the nineteenth century.

Spacecraft

In January 1959, the USSR launched the first craft
intended to come in contact with the moon, called
Mechta. Unfortunately, the astronomers' calcula-
tions were off, and the craft missed its mark by
about 5,000 miles. Two months later, the United
States attempted a similar stunt with the *Pioneer IV*.
It, too, failed to reach the moon.

In 2004, the *Messenger* probe blasted off, hoping
to become the first spacecraft to orbit Mercury in
2011. Why so long a trip? Mercury's orbit speed,
small size, and proximity to the sun makes it
incredibly complicated to plot a "slingshot" route
that will allow for the proper speed and angle to
enter the planet's orbit.

High winds and miscommunication caused *Soyuz
23* to land in a frozen lake, where it broke through
the ice and dragged its two cosmonaut occupants to

the bottom. Divers located the craft and connected it via cables to a helicopter, which dragged it to shore. Thanks to their own survival instincts, the two men inside were retrieved alive.

In 1959, the Soviet spacecraft *Lunik 3* transmitted to Earth photographs of something never previously seen by human eyes: images from the far side of the moon.

On December 15, 1972, Eugene Cernan stepped off the lunar surface and onto the ladder leading up to the *Challenger* module of *Apollo 17*, becoming the last human being (to date) on the moon. His words: "… we leave as we came and, God willing, as we shall return, with peace and hope for all mankind."

The Soviet *Mars 1* space probe was headed to the red planet in early 1963 when it suddenly fell silent about 66 million miles into its journey. It is now believed that mechanical problems caused the failure, but at the time, many were convinced that Martians had attacked or otherwise disabled the craft in order to avoid detection.

When the United States launched the *Pioneer 6* in December 1965, the craft was sent out to orbit the sun and had an expected life span of six months. Incredibly, contact was made with *Pioneer 6* as recently as the year 2000, and parts of it are still thought to be functioning even today.

Spices

While Kentucky Fried Chicken has long promoted its use of 11 herbs and spices in its Original Recipe, those who have attempted to "crack" the secret claim it is merely a combination of five ingredients: flour, salt, sugar, black pepper, and MSG.

Saffron is a slightly bitter, honeylike spice that comes from the crocus plant. It takes approximately 75,000 flowers and about 200 hours of work to produce 1 pound of dried saffron, which is why it's so incredibly expensive at $65 per ounce.

Fathers all across the country have top drawers full of Old Spice cologne and aftershave, long popular as Father's Day gifts. The very first product in the line, however, was Early American Old Spice in 1937, and it was made especially for women.

Despite its name, allspice is not a blend of ingredients; it comes from the berries of the *Pimenta dioica* or Jamaican pepper plant.

The mace you see in the spice aisle at the supermarket has nothing to do with the stuff you spray in the face of an attacker. Mace the spice comes from the same seed that gives us nutmeg, and the two are very similar in flavor.

Countries with hotter climates usually have recipes that call for a lot of spicy ingredients, particularly garlic, onion, allspice, and oregano. These ingredients have significant antibacterial properties, and in the days before refrigeration, they not only flavored meat, but they also prevented it from spoiling.

Sports Equipment

Montreal Canadiens goalie Jacques Plante had worn a protective mask in practice before, but on November 1, 1959, a slap shot shattered his nose and required 200 stitches to repair his face. From that point on, he wore his mask during regular play and became the first NHL goalie to do so.

Prior to the 1893 Army-Navy football game, Navy Cadet Joseph Mason Reeves was told by his doctor that one more blow to the head could prove fatal. Reeves had an Annapolis shoemaker construct a protective leather headpiece and thus became the first football player to wear a helmet.

Andy Bathgate was the first professional hockey player to use a curved stick. Bathgate would heat the blade of a regular hockey stick in hot water, then bend it and close it in the stall door of the men's room until game time to maintain the hook.

The precursor to today's athletic supporter was a rubberized cotton canvas girdle worn by male swimmers in the 1860s. The worsted bathing costumes of that era were too "clingy" and revealing when wet, and the girdle helped to maintain some manly modesty.

The first professional athlete to endorse a piece of sports equipment was Honus Wagner. The Flying Dutchman signed a contract with J.F. Hillerich and Son, manufacturer of the famous Louisville Slugger, in 1905.

Golf balls were originally smooth, but when players noticed that they traveled further after they were worn and scarred, manufacturers started adding the dimples. The number of dimples has increased over the years as mathematicians have figured out more aerodynamic and efficient patterns for them.

Stadiums

Talk about a roofing job! After Hurricane Katrina damaged the Louisiana Superdome in 2005, nearly $200 million was invested in repairs and upgrades, including $33 million to replace 440,000 square feet of the structure's domed roof.

New York's Polo Grounds had the distinction of being the only stadium to host the home games of three different major league franchises: the Yankees, Giants, and Mets.

In 1986, when it was time to place new artificial turf in Bronco Stadium at Boise State University, athletic director Gelln Bleymaier arranged for the fake grass to be installed in the school's colors: blue for the main field and orange for the end zones. Opposing players have admitted difficulty adjusting to the "Smurf Turf," as it is affectionately known.

Only one pro baseball franchise has not changed ballparks at least once. The Florida Marlins have played their home games at Dolphin Stadium (formerly known as Joe Robbie Stadium and Pro Player Stadium) since they became a National League expansion team in 1993.

On November 22, 2003, despite below-zero temperatures, a record crowd of more than 57,000 fans gathered at Edmonton's Commonwealth Stadium to watch first an alumni game and then the first outdoor game in NHL history. The hometown Oilers fell to the Montreal Canadiens 4–3.

No Super Bowl team has played the game in its home stadium. The closest to that was in Super Bowl XIV in 1980, when the Pittsburgh Steelers defeated the Los Angeles Rams at the Rose Bowl in Pasadena, about 15 miles away from the Rams' home turf at Los Angeles Memorial Coliseum, which is where the first Super Bowl was held in 1967.

Star Trek

DeForest Kelley was the first regular cast member of the original *Star Trek* series to pass away, but not before he portrayed a 137-year-old Dr. Leonard "Bones" McCoy in the premiere episode of *Star Trek: The Next Generation* in 1987.

Gossip columns reported that Leonard Nimoy (Mister Spock) threatened to leave *Star Trek* unless he was given a larger dressing room. He relented after producers told him they'd simply "put the ears on someone else."

The three colors of the Star Fleet uniforms appearing in the original *Star Trek* series had a specific meaning. Command, navigation, and weapons control personnel wore gold shirts; engineering and security personnel wore red ones; and medicinal and science personnel wore blue ones. The gold and red shirts flipped significance in all subsequent series except *Enterprise*.

According to series creator Gene Roddenberry, the real life reason Klingons appeared more human-like in the original *Star Trek* series than they did in the subsequent TV sequels and movies was strictly due to budgetary restraints that prevented the development of the elaborate "look" he was hoping for.

Spock was the only actor to appear in every episode of the original *Star Trek* series, including the original pilot. His family name was never revealed on the show, although viewers learned that his parents were the Vulcan Sarek and the human Amanda.

Walter Koenig was added to the *Star Trek* cast for the second season as Ensign Pavel Chekov in hopes that he would help draw younger viewers to the show. He was chosen for the role because he resembled one of the biggest young stars of the late 1960s: Davy Jones of The Monkees.

Space Services, the company that blasted a vial of the late Gene Roddenberry's ashes into space in 1997, performed the same trick with the ashes of James Doohan, who portrayed Chief Engineer Montgomery "Scotty" Scott, 10 years later.

Stars Who Avoided Military Service

In 1967, newspapers reported that The Monkees' Davy Jones escaped being drafted because he was the sole support of his family. In his autobiography, however, he admitted he spent weeks fasting to make himself underweight; the trick worked when he failed his physical.

While many Hollywood celebrities enlisted in the U.S. military following the attack on Pearl Harbor, John Wayne received a deferral because the budding star was the sole support of his family.

After filming only four episodes as the beatnik Maynard G. Krebs in the TV series *The Many Loves of Dobie Gillis*, Bob Denver was drafted into the U.S. Army in 1959. He failed his physical, however, due to a childhood neck injury that had failed to heal properly.

Muhammad Ali originally was classified as 1-Y (not qualified for service) because he'd failed the pre-induction mental examination. As the war escalated, however, he was reclassified as 1-A. He ultimately was granted conscientious objector status as a member of the Nation of Islam.

Actor George Hamilton received a deferment from military service on the grounds that he was the sole support of his divorced mother. It probably didn't hurt his case that his girlfriend at the time was Lynda Johnson, daughter of then-president Lyndon Johnson.

Richard "Cheech" Marin escaped the draft when he relocated to Canada in 1968. He settled in British Columbia, where he first met the man with whom he'd go on to form a successful comedy act: Tommy Chong.

Statues

Which U.S. city has more statues on public display than any other? It's our nation's capital, Washington, D.C., where you can see nearly 100 of them.

The first animated feature film in history, Walt Disney's *Snow White and the Seven Dwarfs*, took three years to complete and cost $1.5 million, a huge sum at the time. The Academy Awards honored Disney for his effort with a unique set of Oscars: one normal-sized statuette and seven tiny ones.

The rumor that the fate of a horseman depicted in a statue is referenced by the number of hooves shown to be off the ground is just that, a rumor. No such pattern exists amongst the majority of equestrian statues.

While Frédéric Auguste Bartholdi designed the Statue of Liberty, the interior frame that supports it was put together by Gustave Eiffel. His name should sound familiar, as he was the man behind that famous Paris landmark, the Eiffel Tower.

Just six months before 9/11, the Taliban made world news by destroying two ancient statues of Buddha in Afghanistan after deeming them offensive.

Abraham Lincoln is actually depicted on *both* sides of the U.S. penny. Not only is his profile on the obverse, but you can also see his marble statue peeking through the columns in the center of the Lincoln Memorial on the back of the coin.

Steel

In order to save other metals for war production, U.S. pennies minted in 1943 were made of steel and, as a result, are attracted by magnets. A handful of 1944 cents were also struck on steel as well.

Is it *Steel* or *Steele?* Here's a short list with the proper spellings: TV detective Remington Steele, author Danielle Steel, pro wrestler George "The Animal" Steele, British politician David Steel, writer Sir Richard Steele, movie executive Dawn Steel, and computer scientist Guy Steele.

What is it that makes steel stainless? A 10 to 30 percent level of chromium in the alloy provides the corrosion resistance necessary to prevent discoloration.

Evidence suggests that the Chinese were able to produce heat-treated steel implements 2,000 years ago. Most of the rest of the world didn't catch on for nearly a millennium.

The logo of the NFL's Pittsburgh Steelers features three colored "hypocycloids," each representing a material associated with steel production: yellow (for coal), orange (for iron ore), and blue (for steel scrap).

Recent tests made on steel samples taken from the *Titanic*'s hull reveal that it had a low manganese content, which makes steel more brittle. Scientists believe this inferior metal was one of the factors that caused the ship's demise.

Stephen King

Some feel Stephen King jinxed Boston Red Sox relief pitcher Tom "Flash" Gordon with his book *The Girl Who Loved Tom Gordon*. After an All-Star 1998 season, Gordon injured his arm in 1999 (just weeks after King's book hit shelves), forcing him to undergo surgery and miss the entire 2000 season. He's bounced around five different ball clubs since.

Stephen King's wife, whom he wed in 1971, has an appropriately bewitching first name: Tabitha.

In interviews, Stephen King revealed the source of inspiration for Paul Sheldon's typewriter in *Misery* missing the letter "n"—the same letter was broken on the author's first typewriter.

Many of King's novels and stories take place in his home state of Maine, notably in the fictional town of Derry.

After watching other directors bring several of his stories to the silver screen, King tried his own hand at it in 1985, when he turned his short story "Trucks" into the motion picture *Maximum Overdrive*. The movie tanked.

The author was severely injured (including a shattered leg and a collapsed lung) when struck by Brian Smith's minivan while taking a walk near his home in Lovell, Maine, in 1999. A few months later, he reportedly bought the Dodge Caravan that hit him and had it destroyed.

Based on a Stephen King novella, many believe that the odd title *The Shawshank Redemption* kept the 1994 motion picture from becoming a much bigger success. Of course, the story's original title, part of the *Different Seasons* compilation, was "Rita Hayworth and the Shawshank Redemption," which wouldn't have been any better.

Stevie Wonder

Wonder's legal name is Steveland Morris, but the singer was born with the last name Judkins. He changed the name to Morris after his mother remarried.

So who was responsible for giving Stevie his Wonder-ful stage name? Motown Records founder

Berry Gordy Jr. christened the youngster "Little Stevie Wonder" when he signed him to the label in 1963.

Stevie's mother was understandably afraid to allow the blind youngster to play outdoors, so she worked to ensure that she found other things to help him bide his time—typically, musical instruments. He proved a "natural" at music and became proficient on many instruments, notably harmonica and piano.

Stevie has been in the music business 45 years, but he's not as old as you might think. He was born in 1950 and had his first chart hit ("Fingertips, Part 2") at the age of 13.

The Miracles' Ronnie White is responsible for getting Stevie his audition with Motown Records. Wonder repaid the favor by cowriting the music for one of the Miracles' biggest hits, "Tears of a Clown."

It's thought Stevie wasn't blind at birth; he lost his sight after only a few hours' exposure to the outside world. Reports vary as to the root cause; some blame problems with the hospital incubator, while others state he was born with underdeveloped eyes.

The Sun

The first Sun Bowl game, held in 1934, involved two high school teams. The event proved such a success for El Paso that they repeated it the following year with college teams. Now called the Brut Sun Bowl, the game was also known as the John Hancock Bowl from 1989–1993.

Sunspot activity peaks about every 11 years, with the next "outbreak" predicted to occur in 2012. With increased activity already seen, some astronomers believe that the sun is more active now than it has been at any point over the last millennium.

In the first incarnation of the comic book character, The Incredible Hulk's transformations were controlled not by his temper but by the sun. Dr. Bruce Banner turned into his gray and later green alter ego at dusk and changed back again at dawn.

The "SPF" code used to measure the power of sunscreen stands for "Sun Protection Factor." The number is intended to multiply (by 10) the number of minutes one can be exposed to the sun without burning. SPF strengths above 30 provide only marginally better protection.

The sun, not the direction of travel, dictates the location of the "tail" of a comet. The solar wind pushes the tail directly away from the sun, and so—depending on its path—a comet may actually follow its tail.

The British tabloid known as *The Sun* contains the same types of celebrity-ripping headlines seen in

American trash mags, with one notable difference: Page Three, which features a photo of a naked woman in each issue.

Helium was first identified in the sun's atmosphere during an 1868 solar eclipse, more than 20 years before scientists discovered that the element also existed here on Earth. The name Helium is based on the Greek word *helios*, meaning "sun."

Superman

The Man of Steel celebrated his birthday on a most unusual day: February 29. No wonder he could "leap" tall buildings in a single bound!

The similarity between the last names of the two most famous actors to play Superman has caused much confusion. For 1950s TV viewers, the man who donned the cape for more than 100 episodes was George Reeves. The actor best known for playing Superman in the 1978 movie version and three sequels was Christopher Reeve (without the "s").

If you want to get your hands on the first comic book featuring Superman, don't shell out a few hundred thousand dollars for 1939's *Superman #1*.

You'll have to pay a cool million (or more) for the issue you're looking for, *Action Comics #1*, dated June 1938.

In 1997, director Tim Burton cast actor Nicolas Cage as the Man of Steel in a then-already-delayed motion picture to be titled *Superman Lives.* The project never got off the ground, and 2006's *Superman Returns* was made with a new script, a new director, and a new lead: Brandon Routh.

Superman co-creator Joseph Shuster wasn't the only talented person in his family. His brother, Frank Shuster of the comedy team Wayne and Shuster, appeared more than 50 times on *The Ed Sullivan Show.*

The DC and Marvel superhero universes crossed over for the first time in 1976 with *The Battle of the Century: Superman vs. The Amazing Spider-Man.* The oversized comic sold for the king-sized price of $2.

Taxicabs

The word "taxicab" is an abbreviated version of its original name, *taximeter cabriolet.* The term was first used for horse-drawn carriages that charged for rides and later applied to automobiles employed for the same purpose.

Checker Motors, long the nation's leading manufacturer of taxis, was one of the very few automakers to really hold its own during the Great Depression.

With fewer Americans able to afford their own cars, the option to call a cab for transportation became more important.

Many sources rank the live audience's reaction to Rev. Jim Ignatowski's repeated utterance, "What does a yellow light mean?" on a 1979 episode of TV's *Taxi* as the longest sustained laugh in sitcom history.

The use of the word "hack" to refer to a cab driver dates back to before the days of automobiles when a "hack" was a horse that one could rent.

Although the term "practice squad" is more commonly used today, sports teams once relied on a "taxi squad" of players that filled in positions during practice or when a player went down due to an injury.

The Harry Chapin hit single "Taxi" was banned from many radio stations, who frowned upon the fact that the song's lyrics told the story of a cabbie who liked "gettin' stoned."

Tea

Tea sets of the eighteenth century featured numbered spoons, which helped the host remember which cup of tea belonged to which guest following a refill.

During film and TV scenes that require characters to drink whiskey, glasses are often filled with watered-down tea instead. It looks the same but keeps the cast alert and sober.

 "I'm a little teapot, short and stout ..." sounds like a Victorian-era nursery rhyme, but the tune was actually written in 1939 by Tin Pan Alley songwriters George Harry Sanders and Clarence Kelley.

Pekoe, as in Orange Pekoe tea, is properly pronounced "peck-oh," not "peek-oh."

According to the Tea Council, the United States is unique when it comes to tea consumption. Of the 50 billion cups of tea we drink annually, 40 billion are served over ice.

The only state that's home to a major plantation where tea is grown commercially is South Carolina. Its American Classic brand has been the official White House tea since 1987.

Rinsing your hands with tea will eliminate food odors, especially fish. The tannic acid in black tea is also said to be effective in removing warts.

Telecommunication

The first cell phone, made by Motorola, measured 9×5 inches and weighed 2½ pounds. The first cell phone call was placed on April 3, 1973, by Dr. Martin Cooper, the General Manager for Motorola's Systems Division.

In the early 1960s, John Draper discovered that a plastic whistle included in boxes of Cap'n Crunch cereal emitted a perfect 2,600 Hz tone. When the Air Force shipped him to England, he was able to make free overseas phone calls by blowing the whistle into the telephone and tripping Ma Bell's long distance trunks.

Mr. Burns on TV's *The Simpsons* persists in answering his telephone with "Ahoy-hoy?" which is one of the greetings that inventor Alexander Graham Bell recommended for his device.

Along Nevada's historic US 50, you'll find the Loneliest Telephone in America. Located about 90 miles east of Reno, the solar-powered payphone can accurately be described as being in the middle of nowhere.

From 1963 to 2003, Jane Barbe "spoke" to some 20 million people per day. Hers was the voice telephone customers heard when they dialed the number for the correct time and also the voice that informed them "the number you have reached is no longer in service."

The "Hello, My Name Is" name tag you see at so many meetings and conferences today was created in 1880 for the first Telephone Operators Convention, which was held in Niagara Falls, New York.

Theme Parks

"America's Oldest Themed Amusement Park" is located in California, but it's not Disneyland. That honor goes to Knott's Berry Farm in Buena Park, whose Ghost Town began attracting visitors back in 1940.

Some mistakenly think that, just as the Dollywood theme park is named after country singer Dolly Parton, Kennywood must be named after country singer Kenny Rogers. In fact, this Pittsburgh landmark—built on land owned by Charles Kenny—has been entertaining customers for more than a century.

Six Flags theme parks are typically divided into six areas related to the flags that have flown over the location of the park. The first in the series was Six Flags Over Texas, honoring the flags of France, Spain, Mexico, the Republic of Texas, the Confederate States of America, and the United States of America.

Kings Island, the popular theme park located in Mason, Ohio (north of Cincinnati), was featured on early-1970s episodes of both *The Brady Bunch* and *The Partridge Family*. Not coincidentally, Paramount Studios was the parent company for both the shows and the park.

Shortly after Disneyland opened in 1955, investors hired away some of the company's executives to head up a new theme park in Denver, Magic Mountain. When financing difficulties occurred, plans were scaled back, and the park closed in 1960 after only a year in business.

Plenty of theme parks sell toys, but one particular chain is *based* on a toy—Legoland parks, which currently operate in Denmark, Germany, the United Kingdom, and the United States.

Opened in 1971, Walt Disney World in Orlando, Florida, remains the largest theme park in the world.

The Titanic

First-class passengers on the *Titanic* paid the equivalent of $124,000 (in 2007 dollars) each for their passage.

The dinner menu in first class on April 14, 1912, was a 10-course affair that included filet mignon, lamb with mint sauce, roast duckling, and sirloin of beef. Third class passengers feasted on rice soup, followed by a main course of roast beef with brown gravy and boiled potatoes.

The "HMS" preceding British ships stands for "Her (or His) Majesty's Ship." The *Titanic*, however, was an "RMS" or "Royal Mail Steamship." During her final hours on April 15, postal clerks desperately tried to save the 200 sacks of registered mail aboard by dragging them to the upper decks.

The Mayflower Curling Rink in Halifax, Nova Scotia, Canada, served as a temporary morgue when ships began returning with the recovered bodies from the *Titanic*. The first victim to be claimed and buried was John Jacob Astor.

The "Unsinkable" Molly Brown, an American socialite aboard the *Titanic*, donned six pairs of wool stockings, a wool suit, fur coat, hat, and muff before leaving her stateroom and heading for the life boats. While rowing toward the *Carpathia*, she passed out most of her garments to the other women to keep them warm.

The Cunard Line, which merged with White Star in 1934, still pays for the perpetual care of the graves of *Titanic* victims.

Toothpaste

About one third of the weight of most toothpaste consists of *humectants* like glycerin or sorbitol. Humectants retain water and help keep the paste soft and pliable.

Many toothpaste brands have since followed suit, but Peak was the first to add baking soda to its formula back in the 1970s.

Mascot Bucky Beaver helped turn Ipana into a popular toothpaste brand (remember the scene in *Grease?*), but sales declined until the mid-1970s, when the brand was discontinued. In an odd twist, Ipana was reintroduced in Turkey in 1991 and has become one of that country's biggest sellers.

Introduced in 1955, Crest became Procter & Gamble's most popular toothpaste, thanks to the addition of fluoride and approval from the American Dental Association. But the company first attempted to break into the market three years earlier with another brand: Gleem.

Inventor Dr. Samuel Zuckerman helped decorate our world. He not only discovered how to add colorful ripples to toothpaste by developing the brand known as Stripe, but he also devised the first high-quality temporary tattoos back in 1981.

Before the days of toothpaste, people used various products to help clean their teeth. In perhaps the most bizarre example, ancient Romans brushed their teeth with human urine. Oddly, urine imported from the Iberian Peninsula was considered better for this purpose than any other.

TV Firsts

The first pay-per-view concert shown on television occurred in 1962. It featured The Kingston Trio performing at Madison Square Garden, and access to the program, using a technology called Phonevision, cost $1.50.

The first company to advertise on television was watchmaker Bulova, whose name appeared on screen for a few seconds preceding a baseball game the afternoon of July 1, 1941, between the Philadelphia Phillies and the Brooklyn Dodgers.

While *Star Trek*'s Captain Kirk and Lieutenant Uhura are widely credited with the first black/white kiss on network television, William Shatner revealed in his autobiography that their lips never actually "met"—it only looked that way on screen thanks to the camera angle.

Telethons have been around since the earliest days of television. Milton Berle hosted the first one on WNBT in New York in 1949, when celebrities gathered to help raise more than $1 million for the Damon Runyon Cancer Fund.

The first television show to utilize "open" captions, that is, captions visible onscreen without special closed captioning equipment, was PBS's *The French Chef.*

Character actress Doris Packer was the first to utter the word "damn" on a network sitcom. She dropped the "d" bomb on an episode of *My Favorite Martian* that originally aired on March 28, 1965.

TV Technology

Radiotelevisione Italia (RAI) in Rome pioneered the use of the "bug," the small corner station/network ID graphic that is now a regular part of the TV experience. Their engineers developed it during the 1970s after discovering that other stations in Italy were "borrowing" and rebroadcasting RAI's programming without permission.

There used to be a channel one on American TV dials, but in 1948, the FCC took some of the VHF (Very High Frequency) bandwidth they'd previously assigned to television and gave it to FM radio. TV had to divide what was left in the 54 MHz to 88MHz spectrum range, which led to the elimination of the lowest channel.

Ampex developed the HS-100 disk recorder, which enabled slow motion instant replay, at the request of ABC. The network first used the technology in 1967 during the World Series of Skiing on *Wide World of Sports*.

Marvin Middlemark invented a V-shaped antenna for television in the 1950s that allowed the viewer to adjust it for the best reception. After 10 years of manufacturing "rabbit ears," Middlemark sold his company for $5 million. Today, consumers wanting to pick up free HDTV programming from local network affiliates use similar antennas.

In 1954, Zenith engineer Gene Polley combined four photocells and a flashlight-like device to make the first television remote control. Polley would later describe the device as the second most civilized invention after the flush toilet.

Even though the FCC approved the NTSC-compatible color TV system in 1953, it wasn't until five years later that one network (NBC) started broadcasting (occasionally) in color. Full-color prime-time programming wasn't offered by all the major networks until 1966.

Underdogs

Mike Tyson had become the youngest heavyweight champion in history in 1986 at the age of 20. He seemed unstoppable until 1990, when an unknown named James "Buster" Douglas overcame 40-to-1 odds and pummeled Iron Mike in a title bout held in Tokyo.

The Colts have never gotten the opportunity to avenge their 1969 loss to Joe Namath and the underdog New York Jets in Super Bowl III. The 1970 NFL-AFL merger placed the Colts in the AFC, the same conference as the Jets, meaning the two teams have to compete for the same slot in the big game.

Having posted a losing record every year since they formed in 1962, the New York Mets weren't optimistic about the 1969 season. Surprisingly, the team won 38 of its last 50 games to win the National League East, and then they defeated the Atlanta Braves and Baltimore Orioles to score an unlikely world championship.

Days before "The Miracle on Ice" at the 1980 Winter Olympics, the Soviet team defeated the United States in an exhibition match by a 10–3 score. When the medal round arrived, however, the Americans stunned the world with a one-goal victory over Team USSR.

The thoroughbred called Man o' War was the odds-on favorite in all 21 races in which he ran, and he won 20 of them. His sole loss was at the Sanford Stakes at Saratoga, to a horse whose name became synonymous with underdog victories: Upset.

Since 1979, the lowest-seeded team to win the NCAA basketball championship was Villanova in 1985. From the eighth position in the Southeast Region, the Wildcats beat Dayton and then upset Michigan, Maryland, North Carolina, Memphis State, and Georgetown to win it all.

Unseen TV Characters

Here's a short list of TV characters who may have been heard but whose faces were never fully revealed on screen.

- Bob Sacamano on *Seinfeld*
- Carlton the doorman on *Rhoda*
- Charlie on *Charlie's Angels*
- Columbo's wife on *Columbo*
- Dorothy's brother, Phil, on *The Golden Girls*
- Karen's husband, Stan, on *Will & Grace*
- Pete's wife, Gladys, on *December Bride*
- Phyllis's husband, Lars, on *The Mary Tyler Moore Show*
- Tim's neighbor, Wilson, on *Home Improvement*
- Niles' wife, Maris, on *Frasier*
- Norm's wife, Vera, on *Cheers*
- Orson on *Mork & Mindy*
- Suzanne's maid, Consuela, on *Designing Women*
- The "Ugly Naked Guy" on *Friends*

U.S. Geographic Anomalies

Hawaii is one of the smallest states in the Union, but it's also the widest. More than 100 tiny, uninhabited islands in the chain stretch 1,500 miles to the northwest of Hawaii's eight main islands.

From downtown Detroit, Michigan, a journey due south will put you in the Great White North; specifically, the town of Windsor, Ontario, Canada.

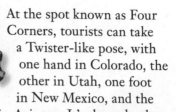

At the spot known as Four Corners, tourists can take a Twister-like pose, with one hand in Colorado, the other in Utah, one foot in New Mexico, and the other in Arizona. It's the only place in the United States where the borders from four states meet.

The District of Columbia was a diamond-shaped area, 10 miles on each side, on the border between Maryland and Virginia. In 1847, the land on the western side of the Potomac River was returned to the State of Virginia.

In 1877, flooding shifted the course of the Missouri river along the Iowa/Nebraska border, leaving the Iowa town of Carter Lake on the "wrong" side of the river. The U.S. Supreme Court eventually ruled that the land still belonged to the Hawkeye State, and today, Carter Lake is the only spot in Iowa on the west bank of the river.

Because Alaska crosses the 180th meridian that separates the Western Hemisphere from the Eastern Hemisphere, it is technically the northern-most, westernmost, and easternmost state in the United States.

Very Long Titles

A few of the longest media titles out there are:

Movies

- *Borat: Cultural Learnings of America for Make Benefit Glorious Nation of Kazakhstan* (2006)
- *Don't Be a Menace to South Central While Drinking Your Juice in the Hood* (1996)
- *Dr. Strangelove, or: How I Learned to Stop Worrying and Love the Bomb* (1964)
- *Everything You Always Wanted to Know About Sex … But Were Afraid to Ask* (1972)
- *The Chronicles of Narnia: The Lion, the Witch and the Wardrobe* (2005)
- *The Incredibly Strange Creatures Who Stopped Living and Became Mixed-Up Zombies* (1964)
- *Who Is Harry Kellerman and Why Is He Saying Those Terrible Things About Me?* (1971)

Songs

- "The Anaheim, Azusa, and Cucamonga Sewing Circle, Book Review and Timing Association" by Jan and Dean
- "Everybody's Got Something to Hide Except for Me and My Monkey" by The Beatles
- "Jeremiah Peabody's Poly Unsaturated Quick Dissolving Fast Acting Pleasant Tasting Green and Purple Pills" by Ray Stevens

- "Objects in the Rear View Mirror May Appear Closer Than They Are" sung by Meat Loaf

- "Several Species of Small Furry Animals Gathered Together in a Cave and Grooving with a Pict" by Pink Floyd

Album

- *When the Pawn Hits the Conflicts He Thinks Like a King What He Knows Throws the Blows When He Goes to the Fight and He'll Win the Whole Thing 'Fore He Enters the Ring There's No Body to Batter When Your Mind Is Your Might So When You Go Solo, You Hold Your Own Hand and Remember That Depth Is the Greatest of Heights and If You Know Where You Stand, Then You Know Where to Land and If You Fall It Won't Matter, Cuz You'll Know That You're Right*, by Fiona Apple

Vice Presidents

Virginia is considered the "home of presidents" because four of the first five U.S. presidents were Virginians. Likewise, New York could be considered the "home of vice presidents." Ten of America's 46 VPs have been New Yorkers, including George Clinton, Theodore Roosevelt, James Sherman, and Nelson Rockefeller.

From 1968–1978, six men held the office of vice president: Hubert Humphrey, Spiro Agnew, Gerald Ford, Nelson Rockefeller, and Walter Mondale. In the 30 years since then, however, only four men have served in that role: George H. W. Bush, Dan Quayle, Al Gore, and Dick Cheney.

In 1990, then–Vice President Dan Quayle appeared on an episode of TV's *Major Dad* to celebrate the 215th anniversary of the United States Marine Corps.

Being second-in-command does not guarantee one a spot in the White House. In fact, when George H. W. Bush won the 1988 presidential election, he became the first sitting vice president since Martin Van Buren (in 1836) to be elected to the higher office.

Frustrated with his efforts to succeed to the presidency, former Vice President Aaron Burr attempted to enlist the help of Mexico in the early 1800s to form his own new nation in the American southwest. He failed there as well.

Two Kings served as vice president of the United States. The first, William Rufus de Vane King, died only six weeks after taking office under Franklin Pierce. The second, Leslie Lynch King, took his adopted father's name.

Gerald Rudolph Ford replaced resigned vice president Spiro Agnew in 1973.

19

Vitamins

Most vitamins are provided by the food we eat, but Vitamin D is different. Some foods (notably dairy products) are typically fortified with Vitamin D, but the human body can produce its own when the skin is exposed to the proper amount of sunlight.

Much ado was made about the fact that, for more than 25 years, Betty Rubble was the only main character from *The Flintstones* who didn't appear in bottles of Flintstone Vitamins. She was finally added to the mix in 1996.

You've most likely heard of B1, B2, B6, and B12, even if you don't play Bingo. Actually, the B-complex is made up of 16 different vitamins.

The short-lived "colorful" versions of Heinz ketchup, first introduced in 2000, only added two things to the condiment's original formula: food coloring and Vitamin C.

Casimir Funk is legendary as the man who coined the word "vitamin," but it was really one big mistake. The name was derived from the Latin *vita-* ("life") and *amine*, since Funk believed them to be nitrogen compounds (amines) that were required for all living creatures to survive.

Most mammals can synthesize Vitamin C (ascorbic acid) in their own bodies, meaning that they are not susceptible to the diseases and conditions that can result from a deficiency. Human beings are a notable exception, meaning we must get our Vitamin C from fresh fruits and vegetables.

Voice Actors

Well before he got his own long-running talk show, millions heard the voice of Mike Douglas. He provided the singing voice of Prince Charming in the 1950 Disney animated feature film *Cinderella*.

Lorenzo Music was a top-notch TV producer, writer, director, and even composer, working on hits like *The Mary Tyler Moore Show* and *The Bob Newhart Show*. He's perhaps best known, however, for his voice-over work, which included the title character in the *Garfield* cartoons.

Parents who watched *The Jetsons* with their kids might have noticed the familiar ring to the voice of mother Jane Jetson. That's because she was portrayed by Penny Singleton, who starred in the title role in more than two dozen *Blondie* movies from 1938 until 1950.

Remember Dwayne Schneider, the handyman on TV's *One Day at a Time?* The actor behind the role, Pat Harrington Jr., donned a French accent to voice the roles of both Inspector Clouseau and assistant Deux-Deux in the *Pink Panther* TV cartoons.

Before he rebounded with *Schindler's List*, Ben Kingsley's career made a precipitous drop in 10 years, from celebrated Oscar-winner (1982's *Gandhi*) to croaking his way through a bizarre amphibian-as-James-Bond cartoon feature (1992's *Freddie as F.R.O.7*).

In the 1968 Beatles film *Yellow Submarine*, the voice of Ringo was performed by Paul. No, not Paul McCartney, but Paul Angelis. The other voices were John Clive (as John Lennon), Geoffrey Hughes (as Paul McCartney), and Peter Batten (as George).

Glenn Close has the distinction of voicing both Tarzan's girlfriend and his mother. She overdubbed Andie MacDowell's speaking parts as Jane in 1984's *Greystoke: The Legend of Tarzan* and then voiced Kala in Disney's animated *Tarzan* in 1999.

The Way We Were

In 1970, movies that contained some adult content were rated "GP" for "General Patronage—All Ages Admitted/Parental Guidance Suggested." The designation was later changed to "PG" to avoid confusion with the more kid-friendly "G."

Gasoline prices peaked at $1.38 per gallon back in 1981. While that doesn't seem like an excessive amount, when converted to 2007 dollars, the adjusted price works out to a number we've become more accustomed to: nearly $3 per gallon.

Prior to 1951, long-distance telephone calls could not be dialed directly; they had to be placed through an operator. Depending on the distance between the two parties, it could take up to 20 minutes for the connection to be made.

PhoneMate introduced its Model 400 answering machine in 1971. The machine weighed about 8 pounds and held 10 minutes worth of messages on a reel-to-reel tape.

When a federally mandated 55 mph nationwide speed limit was established in 1974, many automakers adjusted speedometers to match by changing the usual sequence (10, 20, 30 …) to end in "5" (15, 25, 35 …). The 55 mph point was either shaded or indicated by a special visual mark.

When VCRs first gained popularity in the late 1970s, the units themselves weren't the only expense. The retail price of a single blank video-cassette was initially around $20, while "video club" memberships typically ran in the hundreds of dollars.

Winds

When Volkswagen began working on a new hatch-back model in the early 1970s, it was rumored that the name of the car would be the Blizzard. When it was introduced in 1974, however, the company went with a decidedly opposite name: the Scirocco, after a hot desert wind that blows across the Mediterranean.

Wind chills worsen as the temperature drops. At freezing, a wind blowing 20 mph can bring the wind chill down to a cold but tolerable 20°F. But when the mercury dips to 5°F, the same 20-mph wind makes it feel like –15°F.

The motion picture version of *The Cat in the Hat* wasn't the first disaster related to the Dr. Seuss feline. Back in 1997, during the Macy's Thanksgiving Day Parade in New York, the wind kicked up and blew the balloon *Cat* into a lamppost, the top of which fell and injured four spectators.

Mariah Carey was named for the song "They Call the Wind Mariah" in the musical *Paint Your Wagon*, but the jury's still out on whether it was the 1951 stage version or the 1969 film. *People* magazine claims Mariah is a year older than she says, meaning she was born in March 1969, several months before the film's release.

Thanks to improved weather forecasting, enhanced coordination among authorities, better-built structures, and a bit of luck, tornadoes and hurricanes don't kill as many Americans as they once did. The National Severe Storms Laboratory's list of deadliest tornadoes and hurricanes indicate that none of them occurred in the last 50 years.

Catch the Wind and *Wind Devils* were early titles of a film that went on to become one of the biggest hits in box office history under a much more forceful name: *Twister.* The tornado-chasing movie was one of the first (some sources say *the* first) to be released in DVD format.

Wine

The 1906 San Francisco earthquake had a huge impact on the wine industry. An estimated 25 million gallons of wine were lost in the disaster, including private stashes that were used to help put out fires.

On TV's *Sanford and Son*, old Fred's favorite tipple was Ripple, a fortified wine made by the Gallo brothers. He'd often use it as a mixer, adding it to ginger ale (to make "champipple"), muscatel ("muscatipple"), or créme soda ("cripple").

Champagne was inadvertently popularized by Dom Pierre Perignon, a Benedictine monk who was one of the first to use corks to bottle up his wine.

The carbonation couldn't escape from the bottle, resulting in a bubbly, sparkling wine that took the name of the region of France where it was made.

Wine coolers were all the rage in the 1980s, thanks in no small part to the efforts of David Rufkahr and Dick Maugg. You might know these two by the characters they portrayed: Frank Bartles (the one who spoke) and Ed Jaymes (the one who didn't).

The song "Red Red Wine" was a hit on both sides of the Atlantic. In 1983, the single hit #1 in Great Britain. Five years later, a revamped version topped the charts in the United States. (Neil Diamond wrote and originally recorded it in 1968.)

For most connoisseurs, the old adage that "red wine goes with red meat, white wine goes with white meat" still holds. What's more, scientists have discovered that the chemical reactions set off by matching the right wine with the right meat really can make meals far more pleasurable to the palate.

World Capitals

It's hard to remember the capitals of every one of the world's 193 countries. (After all, Earth was divided into only half as many nations just 50 years ago.) But here are 15 capitals that, for obvious reasons, should be easy for you to file away.

- Algiers, Algeria
- Andorra la Vella, Andorra
- Brasília, Brazil
- Djibouti, Djibouti
- Guatemala City, Guatemala
- Kuwait City, Kuwait
- Luxembourg, Luxembourg
- Mexico City, Mexico
- Monaco, Monaco
- Panama City, Panama
- San Marino, San Marino
- São Tomé, São Tomé and Príncipe
- Singapore, Singapore
- Tunis, Tunisia
- Vatican City, Vatican City

World War II

More than 400,000 American military personnel lost their lives fighting for the Allies during World War II—that's more than the total combined deaths of all those serving the United States in every war before and since.

More than 2 million air raid shelters were constructed in the UK during the first year of World

20

War II. The materials needed to build them were offered for free to households with an annual income under £250.

Which nations suffered the most overall fatalities during World War II? The answer might surprise you. Top on the list is the USSR, with nearly 25 million, followed by China with 20 million. By contrast, Germany and Japan lost 10 million *combined*.

The Tuskegee Airmen, a group of African American pilots who served the United States during World War II, were collectively awarded the Congressional Gold Medal by George W. Bush in a March 2007 presentation.

The Jews weren't the only religious group persecuted by the Nazis before and during World War II. Jehovah's Witnesses were also targeted, and several thousand perished under Adolf Hitler's terrible rule.

World War II affected many facets of life, including snack foods. Hostess Twinkies were originally filled with banana créme, but a shortage of the fruit during World War II caused the company to change to a vanilla-flavored filling.

X, Y, and Z ... a Few Leftovers!

Montgomery Ward is considered the pioneer of the mail-order business. The company's first "catalog" was a single 8×12" sheet that listed 163 different items for sale. Rural customers were the target audience; they were thrilled to be able to order brand-name products and have them delivered locally.

Historians can't seem to agree on the identity of the person who first used anesthesia for surgery. One candidate, Danielsville, Georgia-born Crawford W. Long, reportedly used ether for this purpose back in 1842 but didn't report his discovery until after other physicians had revealed similar successes.

On TV's *Sesame Street*, many of the characters in Bert's life have names that begin with the letter "B." He has a brother named Bart, a nephew named Brad, and a pigeon named Bernice. In an odd twist, he is president of the National Association of "W" Lovers.

In the 1970s, "tear-away" football jerseys became popular wear for college running backs. These lightweight shirts made it easier for a ball carrier to escape from a defenseman's grasp, meaning he'd regularly have to head to the sideline for a replacement. The NCAA banned their use in 1982.

Tang breakfast drink used orangutans in its commercials in 1999–2000, until complaints from animal activists forced Kraft to discontinue what they felt was "exploitation" of the endangered creatures.

The memory capacity of the first IBM PCs was chosen in a rather arbitrary fashion. The Commodore 64 computer had become a success with 64K of memory, so executives felt that 10 times that amount—640K—would ensure the success of the new PC.

About the Authors

Dane, Sandy, and Kara previously collaborated on *The Pocket Idiot's Guide to Not So Useless Facts*.

Dane Sherwood is the author of *Life's Little Destruction Book* and *2,001 Things to Do Before You Die*.

Sandy Wood and **Kara Kovalchik** are the authors of *The Snapple Aptitude Test*. They serve as editors of the infotainment weekly *Tidbits* and are research editors for *mental_floss* magazine.